T0259820

3D Printing with MatterControl

Joan Horvath
Rich Cameron

Apress®

3D Printing with MatterControl

ISBN-13 (pbk): 978-1-4842-1056-7

ISBN-13 (electronic): 978-1-4842-1055-0

Managing Director: Welmoed Spahr
Lead Editor: Michelle Lowman
Development Editor: James Markham
Editorial Board: Steve Anglin, Mark Beckner, Gary Cornell, Louise Corrigan, Jim DeWolf, Jonathan Gennick, Jonathan Hassell, Robert Hutchinson, Michelle Lowman, James Markham, Susan McDermott, Matthew Moodie, Jeffrey Pepper, Douglas Pundick, Ben Renow-Clarke, Gwenan Spearing, Matt Wade, Steve Weiss
Coordinating Editor: Kevin Walter
Copy Editor: Corbin Collins
Compositor: SPi Global
Indexer: SPi Global
Artist: SPi Global

Distributed to the book trade worldwide by Springer Science+Business Media New York, 233 Spring Street, 6th Floor, New York, NY 10013. Phone 1-800-SPRINGER, fax (201) 348-4505, e-mail orders-ny@springer-sbm.com, or visit www.springeronline.com. Apress Media, LLC is a California LLC and the sole member (owner) is Springer Science + Business Media Finance Inc (SSBM Finance Inc). SSBM Finance Inc is a Delaware corporation.

For information on translations, please e-mail rights@apress.com, or visit www.apress.com.

Apress and friends of ED books may be purchased in bulk for academic, corporate, or promotional use. eBook versions and licenses are also available for most titles. For more information, reference our Special Bulk Sales–eBook Licensing web page at www.apress.com/bulk-sales.

Any source code or other supplementary material referenced by the author in this text is available to readers at www.apress.com. For detailed information about how to locate your book's source code, go to www.apress.com/source-code/.

To the MatterHackers team, for believing in open source software

Contents at a Glance

Contents

About the Authors

Joan Horvath and Rich Cameron (known online as "Whosawhatsis") are the cofounders of Nonscriptum LLC based in Pasadena, California. Nonscriptum consults for educational and scientific users in the areas of 3D printing and maker technologies. This book is their latest collaboration, following their earlier works *Mastering 3D Printing* (Apress, 2015) and *The New Shop Class: Getting Started with 3D Printing, Arduino*, and *Wearable Tech* (Apress, 2015). Starting in January 2016, they will also be teaching online classes in 3D printing for LERN Network's U Got Class continuing education program. Links for all of the above are on their website, www.nonscriptum.com.

In addition work with Rich, Joan also has an appointment as Core Adjunct faculty for National University's College of Letters and Sciences. She has taught at the university level in a variety of institutions, both in Southern California and online. Before she and Rich started Nonscriptum, she held a variety of entrepreneurial positions, including VP of Business Development at a Kickstarter-funded 3D printer company. Joan started her career with 16 years at the NASA/Caltech Jet Propulsion Laboratory, where she worked in programs including the technology transfer office, the Magellan spacecraft to Venus, and the TOPEX/Poseidon oceanography spacecraft. She holds an undergraduate degree from MIT in Aeronautics and Astronautics and a master's degree in Engineering from UCLA.

Rich is an experienced open source developer who has been a key member of the RepRap 3D-printer development community for many years. His designs include the original spring/lever extruder mechanism, the RepRap Wallace, and the Deezmaker Bukito portable 3D printer. By building and modifying several of the early open source 3D printers to wrestle unprecedented performance out of them, he has become an expert at maximizing the print quality of filament-based printers. When he's not busy making every aspect of his own 3D printers better, from slicing software to firmware and hardware, he likes to share that knowledge and experience online so that he can help make everyone else's printers better too.

Acknowledgments

The consumer 3D printing ecosystem would not exist in its current form without the open source 3D printing hardware and software community, and in particular this book is a result of the efforts of many developers of the MatterControl software. We are grateful for the support of the MatterHackers team, particular Lars Brubaker, Kevin Pope, and Taylor Landry for their support during the writing of this book. We would also like to acknowledge Marius Kintel, the main developer and maintainer of OpenSCAD software and his collaborators for their software which was used to develop many of the objects in this book. The maker community as a whole has also been very supportive. The picture of Joan and Rich in the "About the Authors" section was taken at San Mateo Makerfaire by Ethan Etnyre; we appreciate all the inspiration we have gotten by looking at projects made by everyone at maker events large and small.

The Apress production team made this process seamless for the most part, and were there with virtual needle and thread for the occasions where it was not. We dealt most directly with Kevin Shea, Michelle Lowman, James Markham, Corbin Collins and Dhanish Kumar, but we also appreciate the many we did not see.

We thank the staff, teachers and students of the Windward School in Los Angeles for inspiration and the use of some of their many great ideas, particularly Regina Rubio, Simon Huss, Lyn Hoge, Cynthia Beals, James Lubin, Geraldine Loveless, and Julie Gunther. We also want to acknowledge the Windward seventh and cigth grade students for showing us what can happen in a classroom; photos of some of their creations are in Chapter 10.

Finally, we are grateful to our families for putting up with our endless brainstorming on the best way to explain some concept or the other. In the same vein, thanks to all of our maker community colleagues who helped us think about a problem, or posed unanswered questions at some point that we have tried to answer here.

Introduction

The consumer 3D-printing landscape has changed a lot in the past year. Initially in the realm of crowdfunded startups, the printers are now starting to look more and more like consumer electronics devices than hobbyist kits. As with any maturing industry, unfortunately along the way there has been a fracturing of standards. Many one-off proprietary systems are coming on to the market. The open source community has been standing against that trend. This book focuses on MatterControl, a program for using any one of the many printers that conform to open source standards.

3D printing can be defined pretty simply: creating an object by building it up layer by layer—rather than by machining it away the way you would by making something from a block of wood or by squirting something into a mold as you would for injection-molded plastic parts. Making 3D printing work, though, is far from simple. 3D-printer designers can take one of two fundamental approaches. Either they can make their system proprietary (using software and hardware available only to them) and tightly control their ecosystem so that the user does not have to (and, often, cannot) make many changes; or they can accept the complexity, requiring that the user be more sophisticated.

This book is aimed primarily at the latter audience. MatterControl hides some of the complexity from users, but also allows flexibility for the printers that support it. MatterControl comes preloaded with settings for some printers, which makes getting started with those printers particulary simple.

This book is meant to be a self-contained tutorial on consumer 3D printers that run open source software. More specifically, it is a "manual plus" for MatterControl and the ecosystem of open source 3D-printing hardware and software surrounding it. We draw on some of the material from the earlier book *Mastering 3D Printing* (Apress, 2014). That book for the most part avoided screenshots and step-by-step instructions because when it was written (about a year before this book), most software interfaces were too much in flux to include in a traditional book. With the maturing of the industry and its software, it is now possible to create more of a step-by-step guide to using particular software. Details may change and features may be added, of course. By the time you read this, MatterControl may have evolved a little, but the fundamentals are now in place. This book is mostly software-focused; if you are more interested in the hardware too and post-processing, you might consider also investing in *Mastering 3D Printing*.

This book can be used as a textbook for a semester-length class or university extension certificate series covering 3D printing and its applications, particularly one focusing on K–12 educators. It might be paired with an in-depth class on 3D computer-aided design (CAD) software for students interested in engineering and industrial or product design, or a group planning on starting with an open source RepRap printer that they plan to modify for specialized applications. Similarly, this book might be paired with a text covering one of the sculptural 3D-modeling programs for students developing skills in 3D animation or fine art.

Part 1 (Chapters 1–3) of the book gives background on the history of these printers, talks about how the hardware works, and introduces the MatterControl software, including downloading and configuring it for a particular printer. Part 2 (Chapters 4–8) is the nitty-gritty tutorial on the workflow of using a 3D printer: developing a 3D model, slicing it into layers that the printer will create one at a time, and controlling the printer in real time. This part concludes with a discussion of special cases, such as printing something hollow. Part 3 (Chapters 9–12) talks about how to put your 3D printer to work, with some case studies, a discussion of classroom lessons learned, and ways of post-processing your 3D print to improve the surface finish. This part reviews creating larger projects and troubleshooting, too. To round out the book, we have two appendices. Appendix A lists the 3D printers currently supported by MatterControl, and Appendix B gathers up all the links referenced in the book so that you can have them in one place.

We hope you enjoy this book and that it launches you on many adventures in 3D printing. As the software and hardware begin slowly mature, we know you will be able to invent and prototype as never before, and we hope in some small way that we can speed you along that road.

PART I

■ ■ ■

The 3D-Printing Ecosystem

Chapter 1 introduces you to desktop 3D printers. Then we move on to talking you through what the MatterControl program is in Chapter 2. Finally, in Chapter 3, we walk you through setting up and installing MatterControl so that you are ready for the 3D printing-workflow in the chapters that follow.

■ ■ ■

The Desktop 3D Printer

Everyone talks about 3D printing, and from all the things you hear about it you would think it was going to solve just about every problem on the planet. The technology is very powerful and has many applications, but it is correspondingly a little challenging to learn to use well. This chapter gives you a little background about the hardware used in 3D printers. Chapter 2 introduces the MatterControl software and discusses how it fits into the (still a little complicated) 3D-printing process. After that, we show you how to install the software, and then you should be off and running!

What Is 3D Printing?

3D printing is more formally known as *additive manufacturing*, since a print is created by making an object one layer at a time, adding on material until it is done. More traditional *subtractive* manufacturing starts off with a block of, say, wood or metal and takes material away as the part emerges. Both techniques shine in certain areas, but 3D printing is particularly useful for creating complex objects, making unique or custom items, or generating prototypes during the design phase of a project.

We could argue that "3D printing" has been around for eons, since every sandbar is built from sand washed up on it. In terms of the lineage of current machines, though, Chuck Hull developed the first 3D printer that used a robotic mechanism to control a laser in about 1984, subsequently commercialized by 3D Systems about five years later. This technique, called *stereolithography* (abbreviated SLA), is still very much in use today, though very much evolved — it uses a laser to solidify an object out of a vat of liquid resin layer by layer.

Since then, other technologies have evolved which can most usefully be organized around the feed stock they use. We give you a quick overview of printers that use powders and resin, which are mostly used in more expensive, commercial applications. Then we move on to consumer, desktop 3D printers that mostly use plastic filament on a spool as feed stock.

Commercial 3D Printers

Many commercial grade printers use one of a set of technologies that we call *selective binding*. These printers fuse a fine powder (such as gypsum, nylon, or even metal) either by using heat to *sinter* or melt the powder particles to fuse them together, or by depositing a binding agent (glue or solvent) to make layers of powder adhere to previous layers. Typically, the process starts by coating an empty build platform with a fine layer of the working powder. Printers have a print head consisting of either a lens and set of mirrors to focus a laser onto the surface of the powder or an inkjet for depositing binding agents onto it. This head fuses one layer's worth of the material at a time, sometimes laying down ink to color the object at the same time. Then another thin layer is laid up on top of this and so on until the print is done. The user has to dig the finished print out of a bed of powder and vacuum off the excess powder. Selective Laser Sintering (SLS) printers work this way, as do direct metal laser sintering (DMLS) and most full-color printers. Printing metal is complex and for some technologies requires filling the build chamber with argon or nitrogen.

3

Another set of technologies uses *selective solidification,* in which a liquid is selectively turned into a solid, typically by using an ultraviolet light source to activate polymerization in liquid resin. SLA (described earlier) was the first example of this, and the Form 1+ printer is a lower-cost example now on the market. Digital light projection (DLP) printers use a projector to harden an entire layer at once. There are now several DLP printers aimed at the consumer market (a search for "DLP 3D printer" on your favorite search engine should give a list). However, the resin hardens when exposed to UV light and requires some care in handling. Managing this makes DLP printers harder to deal with than the ones we are about to describe.

Beyond the printers using plastic, some are being used to extrude food or concrete, and medical printers create tissue substrates for new organs. People have been deploying 3D printers in many applications and size scales. We focus on thermoplastics and similar substances in this book.

▨ **Tip**   We do not discuss commercial 3D printer technologies or go into the history of the current crop of consumer printers further in this book. If you would like more detail, check out Joan's earlier book, *Mastering 3D Printing* (Apress, 2014), which takes a somewhat broader and more philosophical look at the industry than this one.

If you want to learn to maintain your hardware, *Maintaining and Troubleshooting your 3D Printer* by C. Bell (Apress, 2014) is an extremely detailed hands-on review of buying, building, setting up, and calibrating a printer. Bell's book also discusses common firmware choices in detail.

Desktop 3D Printers

The MatterControl program is intended to control 3D printers using a technology variously called Fused Filament Fabrication (FFF) or Fused Deposition Modeling (FDM). This type of machine melts a thermoplastic filament and extrudes it in a sticky, viscous form through a moving nozzle (and/or onto a moving build platform) one thin layer at a time. This extruder works like a high-tech hot glue gun. Layers typically are about 0.1 to 0.3 mm thick. Figure 1-1 shows a few views of a consumer 3D printer building up an object in this way. This type of printer now can be purchased in a variety of configurations, and the rest of this book is focused on these. (The print is a result of the process of 3-dimensionally scanning your trusty author Rich's body and creating a printable object. We describe that process in Chapter 4, but Figure 1-2 shows how the model looked in MatterControl, as a bit of a preview.)

Figure 1-1a. *The first of three shots of a print starting up on a printer. The round spool on the left is a one-kilogram roll of filament*

Figure 1-1b. *Halfway through!*

Figure 1-1c. *All finished*

Figure 1-2. *How the model looked in MatterControl*

Desktop 3D-Printer Hardware

The rest of this book focuses just on filament-based consumer 3D printers, the class that MatterControl supports. In this section we talk through some of their common features and typical designs. There are hundreds of consumer printers on the market, and we cannot be completely exhaustive. Appendix A lists the printers currently formally supported by MatterControl.

Types of Filament-Based 3D Printers

Many different types of 3D printers use thermoplastic filament as the feedstock for 3D printing. Typically the filament comes in spools or cartridges; the printer in Figure 1-1 has a spool next to it on a device that allows it to unspool freely. Chapter 7 discusses different materials and how they are used in printers, but for now the critical thing to know is that most printers work by precisely feeding filament into an *extruder,* which has a cold end that somehow moves the filament and a *hot end* that melts the filament.

The molten material (usually somewhat viscous) then comes out of a nozzle. Nozzle diameters are typically in the range of 0.5 to 0.3 mm. A smaller diameter nozzle does not necessarily mean a print can be of higher resolution; as you will see, there are complex overall design tradeoffs both in the way the printer is built and in the way you elect to use a printer to create something.

Some conventions are common to all printers. For example, they all have some sort of *build platform,* a flat platform on which the print builds up a layer at a time. This platform may be stationary, or it may move in one or more axes. One way or another, material needs to be laid down in three dimensions. Different designers will argue at length about the virtues of different designs, and new ones come out almost daily. We show you a few illustrative examples to give you an idea of the general varieties.

Some design features are common to almost all lower-cost printers. Most use *stepper motors,* which are very reliable and precise motors that move something in predetermined steps—for example, 5 microns at a time. Printers are commonly *open-loop,* meaning they have very limited ability to take corrective action if something goes wrong. If you tell a printer to try to print in thin air, it will do it. This control simplicity makes it easy for hobbyists to create and develop their own printers, but can cause frustrations and add operational complexity.

Cartesian Printers

Many 3D printers are *Cartesian* printers. This means that they are arranged such that they have a frame with three axes at right angles to each other (conventionally called *x*, *y*, and *z*, with the *z* axis being the vertical one).

▓ **Note** If you find this *x*, *y*, *z* convention counter to your intuition, think of it in terms of looking down onto the platform, rather than looking forward into the front of the machine. The *x* and *y* coordinates denote positions on the platform, and the tertiary coordinate (*z*) is elevation from the platform. For screen graphics, it is common to see *x* and *y* denoting coordinates on the screen, with a *z*-index that specifies which object is "on top" in the case of overlap. This was probably influenced by paper 2D graphs, in which the paper would normally be sitting on a horizontal surface, and thus *x* and *y* would both be horizontal. You may find that some 3D modeling packages have different conventions and you may need to rotate your object to get it to lay on the platform the way you intended when you move into MatterControl (as we will discuss in Chapters 4 and 5.)

Figure 1-3 and 1-4 show two different Cartesian printer implementations. Figure 1-3 is a printer that has a stationary platform and an extruder that moves in all three dimensions. It is also a *direct drive* extruder in which the filament is pushed into the hot end with an actuator that is connected directly to the hot end. Figure 1-4 is a Cartesian printer that moves its platform in one axis (the *y* axis, toward you in the picture), moves its extruder from right to left to give movement in the *x* axis, and then the whole *x*-axis is moved up and down to give layer by layer *z* motion. You will notice that a tube comes out of the extruder; this is called a Bowden tube and it guides the filament to the extruder from a drive gear at a distance. Bowden extruders can sometimes give higher performance because less of the mechanism has to be moved around. (As a side note, Rich designed the printer in Figure 1-4 when he was working for the manufacturer.)

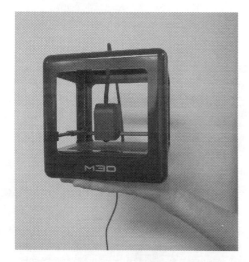

Figure 1-3. *A Cartesian 3D printer with a direct-drive extruder (M3D)*

Figure 1-4. *A Cartesian 3D printer with a Bowden tube on its extruder (Deezmaker Bukito, also used for the pictures in Figures 1-1)*

Non-Cartesian Printers

The other major category of printers are the non-Cartesian printers, the most common of which are delta, or deltabot, printers. These machines are descendants of *pick and place* machines—robots that are used in factories to pick things up and move them around. Deltas have the advantage that their build platforms are stationary, but their extruder movement is very complex. Figure 1-5 shows a deltabot from manufacturer SeeMeCNC. Deltas can also be made very big; Figure 1-6 shows the PartDaddy, a giant deltabot that SeeMeCNC takes to Makerfaires and similar events to show how large parts can be made.

Figure 1-5. *A deltabot (Orion by SeeMeCNC)*

▒ **Tip** If you want to learn more about delta printers in particular, C. Bell's book *3D Printing with Delta Printers* (Apress, 2015) may be a good resource for you.

Figure 1-6. *A huge deltabot (the PartDaddy). Note the difference in scale from the previous printers!*

There are also other designs such as polar printers (in which one or more axes rotate rather than move linearly) and a variety of other experimental systems. Non-Cartesian printers have to convert the Cartesian coordinates provided by slicing software into ones appropriate for their own mechanical systems, but this is typically done internally by the printer's firmware, and is thus mostly transparent to the user. For the most part, these design features will not significantly affect how you would interact with MatterControl, if the software supports them.

3D Printer Options

3D printers are relatively simple robots with a few key components. Most are really just four or more stepper motors, a stiff frame, a microprocessor, and something to heat and control the deposition of the plastic. However, depending on exactly what you are trying to do, you may need to add some additional capability to your printer.

Heated Beds

Some printers have heated build platforms, sometimes called heated beds. One of the challenges of 3D printing is to get the first layer to stick just enough to the build platform. Too little, and the print will get knocked off by the extruder partway through the print; too much, and you might break the print (or even part of the printer) trying to get it off. By delaying the cooling that causes plastic to shrink, heating the bed gives some more control for materials that are difficult to manage. Different manufacturers make their build platforms out of different materials, and what works best depends on a lot of things that you will see in Chapter 7. Generally, though, like most things in 3D printing, having a heated bed adds flexibility at the cost of more complexity.

Multiple Extruders

Some printers have more than one extruder, allowing them to print in multiple materials or colors or to create support material that can be washed away (see Chapters 5 and 8). At the moment, configuring the software for multiple extruders is a little fiddly and requires that you explicitly tell the software things like exactly how far apart the extruders are. We get into this more in Chapters 5 and 6, but some of the configurations you will see in Chapter 3 require you to input some things about the design of your extruders, so we mention it now.

Electronics Options

Many 3D printers run off some variant of an Arduino processor. An Arduino (http://arduino.cc) is an open source (more on this in a minute) microcontroller platform that is relatively easy to program and quite good at controlling mechanisms like stepper motors, heaters, and the other simple devices that make up a 3D printer.

The current baseline for 3D printer controllers is the RAMPS (Reprap Arduino Mega Pololu Shield), which is an Arduino add-on board (known as a shield) that sits between an Arduino Mega and several stepper driver boards made by Pololu. This has spawned compatible boards that integrate the functionality of the RAMPS board and Arduino Mega, some of which have names like RAMBo and RUMBA, while lower-cost designs like the Sanguinololu and Teensylu use smaller microcontrollers with similar capabilities. The Azteeg line of controllers and the Printrboard are common branded controller boards based on these designs.

There are a few different options for firmware to run on these controllers. The firmware receives and interprets a set of commands called G-code (Chapter 6) that control the various functions of the printer. The most common firmware for these boards is called *Marlin,* but any of them should understand the G-code that MatterControl sends.

The Mightyboard is a printer controller designed by Makerbot for the Replicator 3D printer, and used by the Replicator, Replicator 2/2X, and a number of clones of these machines. Mightyboards have similar hardware to a RAMBo or RUMBA, but have their own firmware that uses x3g files instead of G-code. The x3g format includes commands similar to G-code but is a binary format that has some machine characteristics baked-in. If you select the Makerbot option for G-code output, MatterControl will give you the option to convert the G-code it generates to an x3g file.

Some printer controllers are now using more powerful ARM-based microcontrollers. Each of these has its own firmware, but the most popular of these is currently the Smoothie project, which consists of the Smoothieboard and Smoothieware firmware. This firmware is designed to run G-code in a way that is more or less backward-compatible with Marlin.

▓ **Note**   You may have heard people discuss the finickyness of 3D-printer alignment. 3D printers have very high requirements for internally-consistent geometrical accuracy, and printers vary on how difficult it is to keep everything calibrated. MatterControl has some capability to do some automated build platform compensation, which it calls *automatic print leveling.* We talk about that in Chapter 3 where we discuss setting up MatterControl.

Open Source

You will see the term *open source* frequently in this book. *Open source* does not refer to any particular design or standard; it is a way that software and (more recently) hardware is developed by a community that decides it is going to share a design, perhaps based around some standards. Sometimes (as is the case with MatterControl software) most of the development is done by a core team of developers who either are volunteers or who financially support themselves with other things in addition to software development. Typically open source software is free, but you are expected to make anything you add to it free as well. This means that quite large ecosystems can grow up quickly. The opposite of open source is *proprietary*—systems that either are protected by patents or whose working is kept a trade secret. MatterControl works with open source printers and some proprietary ones; Appendix A lists the ones it officially supports.

3D printing for a long time was an entirely proprietary process, controlled by a few companies. Around 2007, key patents started running out. Adrian Bowyer, a researcher in England, decided it would be fun to try to design a 3D printer that could be created out of readily available parts plus some 3D printed ones, thus creating a printer that could (partially) print itself. He also made his designs readily available and encouraged others to build on them. These printers, called RepRaps (for *self-REPlicating RAPid prototypers,* http://reprap.org), very quickly began to evolve into a variety of types. The process was accelerated by the invention of online crowdfunding platforms like Kickstarter (www.kickstarter.com) and Indiegogo (www.indiegogo.com). Many of the designs we have mentioned in this chapter have RepRap lineage.

Several years earlier, the open source Arduino microprocessor was developed by a group in Italy that wanted to have an easy-to-program processor to use to teach electronics. The processor was widely adopted by RepRap printer developers (with some modifications and extensions) and was an enabler there as well. The microprocessor needed some software to allow it to run the code to make models; this software is called *firmware,* and there are several common open source firmware programs, most notably Marlin. This low-cost processor with its open source firmware was an enabler for RepRap printer development.

MatterControl itself is an open source program, curated by MatterHackers (www.matterhackers.com) in Southern California (the team is pictured in Figure 1-7). The program is free, but MatterHackers sells some plugins (Chapter 11) and also sells printers and supplies and provides tech support services for some manufacturers. In Chapter 2 you will see more about the software side of 3D printing, both in the overall process of creating a 3D print and as managed by MatterControl.

Figure 1-7. *Some of the MatterHackers team*

▥ **Note** We are giving just the barest of introductions to open source here. We provide more in-depth information in our book *The New Shop Class: Getting Started With 3D Printing, Arduino and Wearable Tech* (Apress, 2015). There is also more on the topic in Joan's book *Mastering 3D Printing* (Apress, 2014).

Summary

This chapter gave an introduction to 3D printing in general, and to the hardware—the 3D printers themselves. The next chapter introduces the MatterControl software and discusses how it fits into the 3D-printing workflow. The process of using a 3D printer is still a relatively complex one, requiring knowledge of hardware, software, the material you are printing with, as well as how all these aspects interact. The next chapter gives you an introduction to the second of these key pieces: software.

■ ■ ■

CHAPTER 2

What Is MatterControl?

MatterControl is a computer program that allows you to control a large part of the 3D-printing workflow. Using a 3D printer is still a little complex. In some ways, the word *printing* is a little unfortunate, because analogies with 2D paper printing are a little misleading and can lead to assumptions that somehow you just click a Print button somewhere and get a physical object out. The reality is that it is more similar to cooking, and that you need to do a bit of tweaking and know what you are doing, at least a little. MatterControl tries to hide some of the idiosyncrasies of the different printers by having a common user interface. This chapter provides an introduction into what MatterControl does (and also what it does not do) so that you can see how it fits into the overall 3D-printing workflow. We will do a quick walk through all the functionality and then subsequent chapters will go through each aspect in detail.

Why use MatterControl to control your printer? It puts together most of the software you need for the 3D-printing workflow in one place, while giving you a lot of options in controlling your 3D printer and your library of objects. After a while, you will discover that you have collected a lot of things that you have printed and might want to print again, perhaps with some tweaking. MatterControl's library can help with that; we go into it in Chapter 9's section on file management.

MatterControl is an open source program meant to give users maximum flexibility. As we saw in Chapter 1, *open source* means that a community works together to develop and add to the capabilities of the program (in this case, it is curated and mostly developed by the MatterHackers team). *Flexibility,* however, means that the user's job can be more complex if the user takes advantage of that flexibility. In this book we try to first give you the minimal knowledge you need to get started printing and then venture out more into some of the advanced topics, or give you resources to learn more on your own.

The 3D-Printing Workflow

The 3D-printing process consists of three steps: creating a 3D model, changing that model into a file that can be executed on a 3D printer (a process known as *slicing*), and finally loading the model on the printer and having it print. The slicing process, as Chapter 5 describes, requires that you think about the physicality of the printer: what material you are using, what might make the print fall apart when the machine is building it, and so on.

When people use a 3D printer for the first time, they are often taken aback a bit by how steep the learning curve is. If you realize that you have a small factory on your desk, then perhaps it might make more sense that there is some significant complexity to think through. You are designing the shape of a 3D object, deciding what material to make it out of, and setting up a little factory to produce one robotically.

In the case of consumer 3D printers, the robot is not all that smart, either, so you need to anticipate what might get it confused and allow for that in your planning. Figure 2-1 gives an overview of the workflow; we walk through it quickly here with some pointers forward to upcoming chapters. Figure 2-2 shows you a typical MatterControl home screen at the start of the process.

Figure 2-1. 3D-printing workflow

▓ **Tip** If you are still debating whether to buy a 3D printer and are reading this book to see what is involved, do not be discouraged by all this information. Once you have your hardware in front of you and start working through the examples in later chapters, you will develop some intuition. That said, be sure you read reviews of printers before buying one, and see what their tech support reviews say in particular. Many printers are still sold as kits of varying complexity; be sure you are comfortable with electronics before going that route. If you live near a hackerspace or makerspace with installed 3D printers, you might try visiting and talking to people there about their experiences.

Be aware that MatterControl is designed for *open source* printers (see Chapter 1), which have elected to use certain non-proprietary standards and to put their improvements out publicly as well. Some common brands of printer are not open source and have their own proprietary workflows, so if you like the look of MatterControl, be sure to check whether it is compatible or not before buying a printer. Some printers have a custom version of MatterControl that does some of the setup described in Chapter 3 for you. Appendix A lists printers that are supported at various levels by the MatterControl team, or you can check with the printer manufacturer.

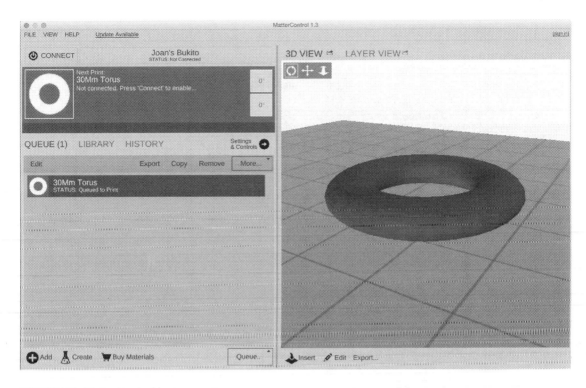

Figure 2-2. *MatterControl home screen*

Step 1. Obtain a 3D Model

The 3D-printing process starts with a 3D model. You can download an existing model from one of the databases that are out there, modify one of those models, or create a new one yourself. You can also use a 3D scanner, although 3D-scanning technology is still a little hard to use at the consumer level.

If you choose to create your own model, you will need to use a 3D design package (not just a 2D drawing program). There are many free models and software packages out there for you to explore before you start buying anything. If you are already an expert 3D modeler, of course, you can use the program you are used to if it can create the correct type of file (STL or AMF, as we discuss shortly) or a file that can be translated into it. Chapter 4 goes through the options for all of these in detail.

3D Model File Formats

The term *3D computer model* is used in many different contexts — which can cause confusion when someone wants to print something using a 3D printer. In this book, *3D computer model* means a computer file that contains enough information about the surface of an object to allow the object to be printed. In the open source consumer 3D-printer world, the most common file format is the STL file. This acronym is sometimes said to stand for *STereoLithography* and sometimes for *Surface Tesselation Language*.

STL is something of a lowest-common-denominator file format, consisting essentially of a long list of triangles that collectively cover the surface of the object. It is not a terribly efficient format (particularly in its ASCII version, which is a text file), but it has the virtue of being relatively simple to generate and deal with and therefore has become a de facto standard. STL files only contain information about the shape of the surface. No information about color is contained in an STL file.

STL standards exist for both ASCII and binary file versions. For 3D printers with multiple extruders capable of printing in multiple colors or materials, an AMF file (which stands for Additive Manufacturing File format) is used.

On a Windows computer, you may get an error when saving or moving around an STL file. On Windows, the STL filename extension is presumed to mean Certificate Trust List, and STL files will show up that way in directory listings. STL files will work with 3D-printing programs on Windows machines, but sometimes opening the file or saving them will result in an error message complaining about Certificate Trust Lists.

▦ **Tip**   The open source program MeshLab (available at `http://meshlab.sourceforge.net`) is able to translate many different types of files into STL. It can also fix the problems that sometimes occur during translation or as a result of printing incompatibilities in the original model itself. Opening the program, importing the mesh, and exporting it again solves many problems. The free Meshmixer app from Autodesk (`www.123dapp.com/meshmixer`) can also fix a lot of problems and in addition can cut an object in half and otherwise do minor modifications that can be very handy sometimes.

What Does "Watertight and Manifold" Mean?

Models for 3D printing need to be *watertight* and *manifold*. A *watertight* object, as the name implies, does not have holes in its surface. A *manifold* object means that every triangle edge is shared by two and only two triangles, and no triangles intersect except along their edges. Sometimes a solid object will be created in such a way that there are several "objects" or parts of the same object sharing the same space, which will confuse matters later on.

You may be able to use the MeshLab program noted in the preceding tip to correct the problem of objects in the same space, and slicing software is slowly getting better at fixing this during the slicing process. Models that are not watertight and manifold may generate errors later in the "slicing" part of the process, which is summarized in the next section and covered in detail in Chapter 5.

Sometimes, though, the slicing software just "does something" to try and fix problems; if you see weird geometries when you look at the preview of your print, you may have a print with holes or that is non-manifold. You can try to clean it up and slice it again.

▦ **Note**   A variety of other 3D-modeling formats have evolved in specific industries and for particular modeling needs. This book focuses on the STL format. Should you find yourself with a different file format, a quick online search will usually reveal a translation program. The other common format, OBJ, is similar to STL but also preserves color (and some other) information. To use an OBJ file with MatterControl, you need to convert it using MeshLab (see previous Tip) or other conversion program.

Step 2. Slice the 3D Model

Once you have a model in STL or AMF format, bring it into MatterControl's queue by clicking the Add button on the home page. The next step in the 3D-printing process is to *slice* the STL (or AMF) file. 3D printers build up a model layer by layer; the slicing process, as the name implies, takes the 3D surface model in STL format and converts it into commands that can move the printer's mechanical parts. These commands are called G-code. Figure 2-3 shows a file that was generated in Tinkercad (see Chapter 4) that has just been imported into MatterControl. It's a small keychain that Chapters 4–6 look at closely.

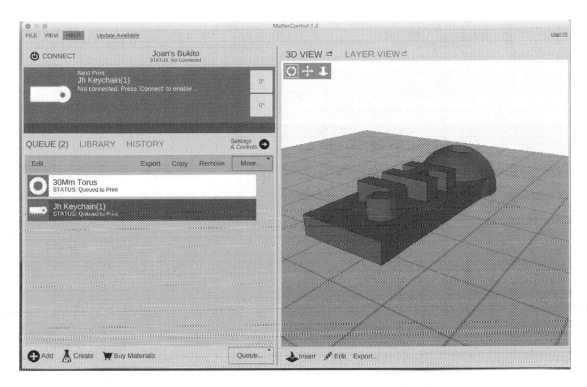

Figure 2-3. *Bringing a file into MatterControl*

Slicing also has to take account of the material being used for printing, some physical and software characteristics of the 3D printer, and some things about the model's geometry. Chapter 5 goes into the slicing process in great detail.

MatterControl gives you a choice of three *slicing engines*, programs that go about the process a bit differently. As you go forward, you may find you like one better than the other for certain kinds of prints. For now, you can use MatterSlice as a default. You select the slicing engine to be used on the OPTIONS screen, described in Chapter 3.

Step 3. Reviewing the Sliced File and Printing

Once you have loaded a 3D model into MatterControl and sliced it, you will have a G-code file (see Chapter 6 for a lot more on G-code). That file can be viewed in the Layer View window (if the file has not been sliced yet, click Generate to see the layers). Chapter 6 discusses a variety of options for viewing the layers to be printed; essentially, you can animate and preview what the print head will do ahead of time—how the plastic will be laid down, as well as how the print speed may vary, and when the printer will be pulling back the filament to leave spaces in the print (known as *retraction*).

It is always good to go through the animation carefully so that you do not waste a lot of time if your model did not slice correctly. (As we will note shortly, 3D prints can take a very long time.) Figure 2-4 shows the layers in our keychain print in 3D. The blobs above the actual print are points where the filament was being pulled back to leave a space; the big blob is the point where the filament is pulled way back away from the print at the very end.

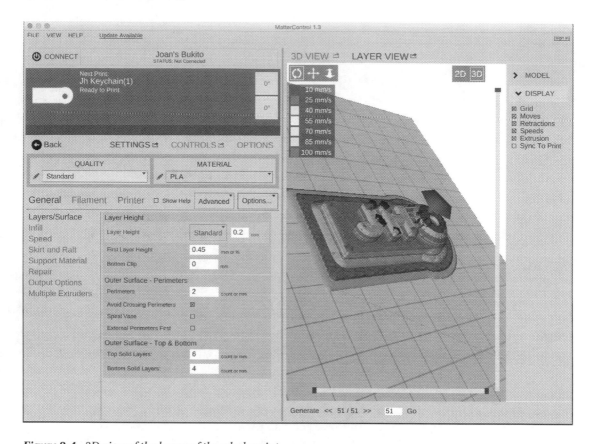

Figure 2-4. *3D view of the layers of the whole print*

Figure 2-5 is a 2D view of one layer partway done (the slider on the bottom controls how far you are through a layer; the one on the side selects the layer). Being able to move around virtually within a print is very powerful, because sometimes a 3D model has subtle problems that are not handled correctly by later steps in the process, and you can avoid wasting materials and time by seeing what will happen first. The visualizations are not perfect.

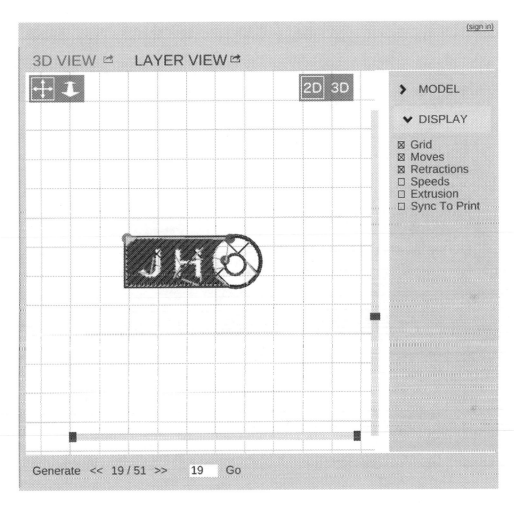

Figure 2-5. *View of one partial layer in mid-print*

For example, if you create a situation where the printer will be trying to print in midair because you forgot to put in a supporting structure below an overhanging area, the simulation will just show it printing just fine in midair. Using this Layer View can help you catch other common problems as we will discuss in detail in Chapter 10.

Besides visualizing what the printer is going to do, you can also use MatterControl to move the physical printer hardware. You can also use the capabilities under Settings & Controls ➤ CONTROLS to move the print head or adjust temperatures during the print. Chapters 6 and 7 talk about why and when you might want to do that.

MatterControl's Capabilities

MatterControl is able to manage the slicing and execution parts of the process, as well as manage your library of objects. To import into the queue (immediate slicing and loading) use the Add button. To store a file for later or for archival purposes, click Library ➤ More ➤ Add To Library. Chapter 9 discusses file management in more detail.

MatterControl does not include a full-blown design program, but it does allow you to make an object you have brought in from an outside program bigger or smaller, and to rotate it so that it prints more easily. MatterControl also allows you to merge two objects into one. Chapter 11 talks more about add-ons to these basic capabilities. Currently MatterControl includes a plugin called TextCreator, shown in Figure 2-6, that allows you to create objects made of letters. You can purchase an add-on plugin as well that lets you print flat stencils from 3D images. This capability is accessed from the Create icon at the bottom of the home screen.

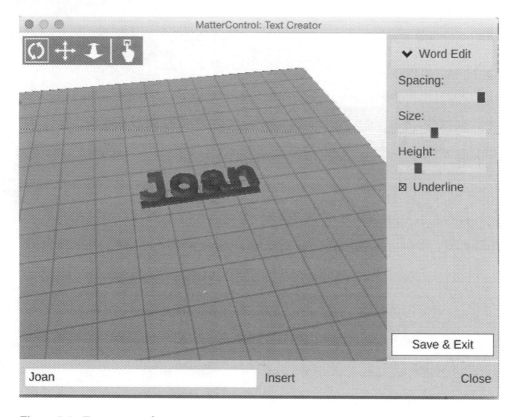

Figure 2-6. *Text creator plugin output*

Using an SD Card

Your printer may come with an SD card reader. SD cards are the cards in some cameras that store pictures until you can copy them to a computer. You can save files from MatterControl onto an SD card inserted into your laptop. Check your manufacturer's instructions to see whether the file needs to be named something in particular to be recognized, or use the LCD interface on your printer to select the file to print.

The MatterControl Touch Tablet

MatterControl also runs on a dedicated tablet (see Figure 2-7), called the MatterControl Touch, available from MatterHackers. Using the tablet lets you have more insight into what your printer is doing than you would from just running off an SD card without tying up a computer for the duration. Chapter 9 discusses the Touch and its capabilities in more detail.

Figure 2-7. *The MatterControl Touch tablet*

A Note about 3D Print Durations

You may be wondering why 3D-printer manufacturers highlight that their machines are able to run from an SD card versus just being plugged into a computer, or why you would want a dedicated tablet to run your printer. The reason is that 3D prints typically take a long time—often many hours, if not days. Having a computer plugged in for that amount of time first of all ties up the computer and secondly can be the cause of a failed print if the computer goes to sleep or needs to be restarted (such as for system updates, which Windows computers in particular have been known to do without warning).

Printers typically just download a few commands at a time from their hosts, so if anything glitches, you may lose many hours of printing. Most consumer 3D printers cannot restart; you need to throw out the print and start over. Given this state of the art, anything that isolates the printer a bit and also avoids tying up a laptop or other computer is a good thing.

You can also often save yourself a lot of grief by using the 3D view features carefully, looking at what you will print ahead of time, and adjusting settings (see Chapters 5 and 6) if you do not like what you see. This view also gives you an estimate of how much time and filament the print will take. The time estimate may be a little off (it is likely a little low) but will give you some feedback about how much time you might save if you play with some of the optional parameters we cover later.

People who are used to tradional machining are often surprised by how *fast* a low-cost consumer 3D printer is for complex shapes, since milling something out of a big piece of metal is not all that fast either. However, most consumers are more used to 2D paper printers than to computer-controlled milling machines, and so that is the comparison that gets made (somewhat unfairly).

Summary

This chapter gave an overview of the 3Dprinting workflow and discussed where MatterControl fits into it. It also went over a few key issues about 3D printing, like speed of printing and the implications of very long print times. The next chapter covers downloading and setting up the MatterControl software for your particular printer. Subsequent chapters get into the detailed steps involved in 3D printing with MatterControl.

CHAPTER 3

■ ■ ■

Downloading and Configuring MatterControl

As discussed in the last chapter, MatterControl is a free, open source software package. To download it, go to and click the Download link, `http://www.mattercontrol.com/#jumpMatterControlDownloads`. Once you are on the Download page, select the Windows, Mac, or Linux installer version as appropriate for your computer (the type of 3D printer you have does not affect what you download). MatterControl is supported on Mac OS X 10.7 and higher, Windows Vista and higher, and either Ubuntu or Mint Linux. MatterControl now also supports touchscreen interaction on its tablet, the MatterControl Touch.

■ **Note**   In this book we show screenshots of MatterControl running on a Mac using the version of OS X that is current as we write the book (10.10 or higher). There may be small variations in the Windows and LINUX versions.

Once you have downloaded the MatterControl installer, locate it in your download folder and run the installer. Follow the onscreen instructions. At the end of the installation, you will be prompted to run your new installation of MatterControl.

■ **Tip**   As mentioned in Chapter 1, your 3D printer may use a number of different controller boards. MatterControl works transparently with controller boards that run standard G-code (explained in Chapter 6) and that communicate over a serial port with the printer. In order to communicate with the printer, your computer needs the appropriate serial driver. Many boards now work with built-in drivers on most operating systems, but if yours does not, you may need to install a driver before you can establish communication. Notably, the RAMBo controller requires a driver to be installed under Windows, so if your printer has a RAMBo, and you are on a host computer running Windows, you may need the instructions found at `www.matterhackers.com/articles/installing-rambo-driver`.

Getting Started Using MatterControl

Once you have installed the software, you can start it up. You should see a screen like the one in Figure 3-1. This section walks you through the key options on this home screen, starting with connecting your printer and configuring the software. We call this view the *home screen* or *main menu*.

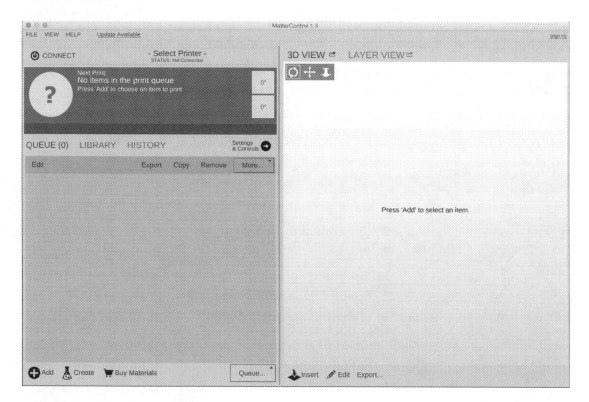

Figure 3-1. *The MatterControl home screen*

MatterControl Home Screen

In the upper left, you see the Select Printer box. Click that, and the dialog box shown in Figure 3-2 will pop up. Give your printer a name (like "Joan's Printer" or "Bukobot #5") that will let you know which one you are referring to. Select the make and then the model of your printer from the dropdown menus and follow the instructions to connect.

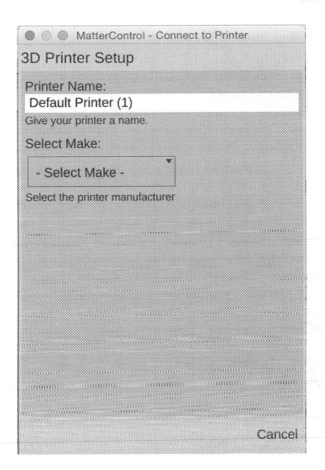

Figure 3-2. *Select Printer dialog*

If your printer is not listed, you will need to tell MatterControl a few important pieces of information about your printer. Select Other ➤ Other and you will be asked to select a baud rate so that MatterControl can establish a serial connection. If your printer fails to connect, try the other options until one connects. Then (being sure you have selected a printer) go to the Settings & Controls ➤ SETTINGS ➤ Printer item to bring up the settings shown in Figure 3-3 and 3-3b. The examples here show the manufacturer's settings for one particular printer; if your manufacturer supplies nothing, enter the dimensions of the usable area of the print bed, coordinates of the center of the bed (usually half of each dimension), and the maximum usable build height, all in millimeters. If you are using a Cartesian 3D printer, the bed shape is almost certainly rectangular. With a delta or polar printer, your platform should be circular, and you should use (0,0) as the print center.

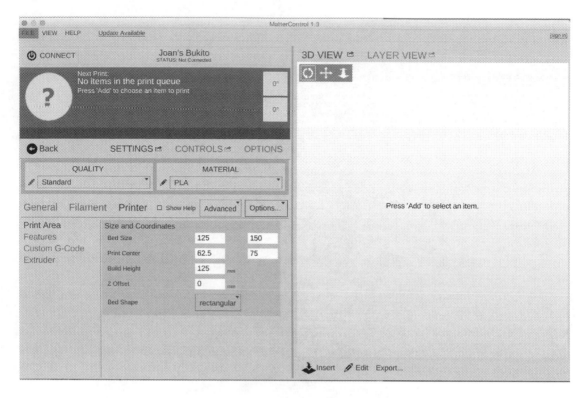

Figure 3-3a. *SETTINGS ➤ Printer ➤ Print Area screen*

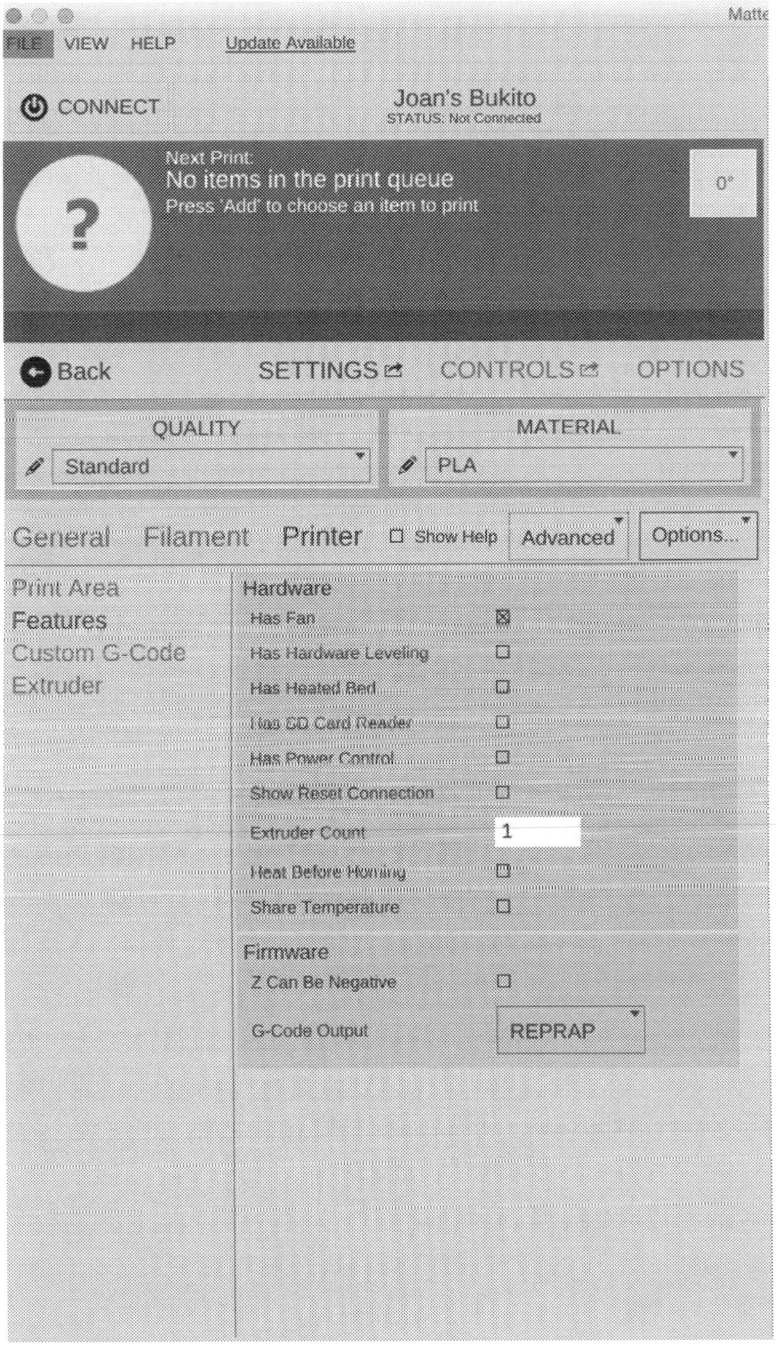

Figure 3-3b. *SETTINGS ➤ Printer ➤ Features screen*

For the rest of this list, check any boxes that apply to your printer and leave them unchecked if they do not apply or if you are not sure. Leave RepRap selected in the Gcode Output menu unless your printer matches one of the other types listed in that menu (for example, if you have a Makerbot clone, such as one of the FlashForge machines, choose Makerbot). Next, click Extruder on the left and enter the diameter of your nozzle in the first box (typically 0.3–0.5 mm).

Whether MatterControl came with settings for your printer or not, you also need to switch to the Filament section and enter the diameter of your filament in the first box. Your extruder is designed either for 1.75 mm or for 3 mm filament, but due to an accident of history, most "3 mm" filament should actually be closer to 2.85 mm in diameter, and MatterControl needs to know the correct value in order to properly print your object. The default temperatures are for PLA, (polylactic acid, one of the common printing materials) but if you're starting with something else, you can set the temperatures for that here as well. Chapter 7 goes into materials selection in detail.

▓ **Note**   There are a lot of other knobs to fiddle with in the slicing settings, which Chapter 5 discusses in more detail, but the rest of MatterControl's defaults should be sensible for most machines. If the Custom G-Code section is blank, leave it that way for now and revisit it after you read Chapters 5 and 6. Meanwhile, there is a check box at the top of the SETTINGS panels labeled "Show Help." By clicking the box, you can get short descriptions of the functions of each slicing setting displayed directly.

OPTIONS Menus

Now that you have told MatterControl which printer you will be using, there are a few other things for you to set up. You will see three clickable headings across the top: SETTINGS, CONTROLS, and OPTIONS. We talk about the first two later in the book, particularly in Chapters 5 (for SETTINGS) and 6 (CONTROLS). This section walks you through the variables listed under OPTIONS. Figure 3-4 shows the OPTIONS screen.

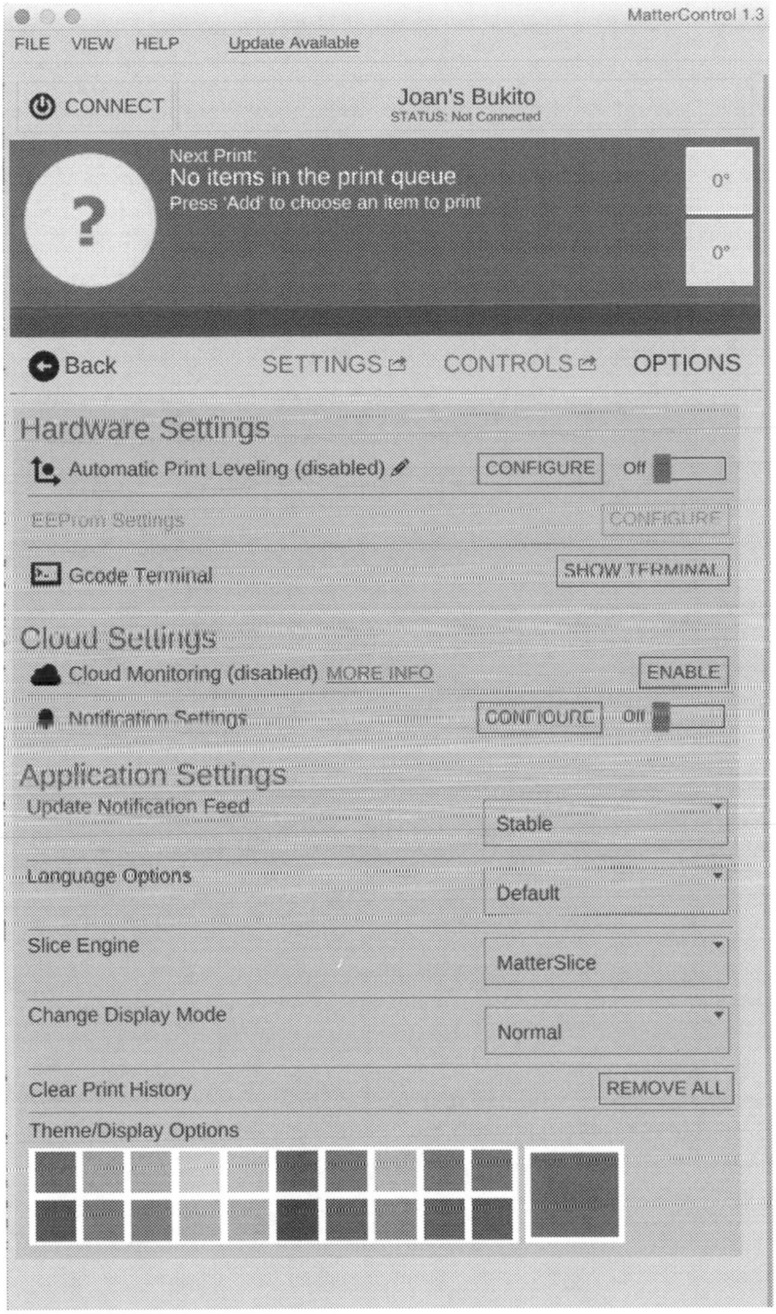

Figure 3-4. *The OPTIONS screen*

Hardware Settings

The first group of settings affects how MatterControl interacts with your printer hardware and provides a way to look at the detailed commands that are sent to the printer to aid in debugging if things are not going well.

Automatic Print Leveling

When using any printer, it is critical that your first layer is parallel to the build platform so that the plastic will stick. *Automatic Print Leveling,* also known as *Automatic Bed Leveling* or simply *auto-leveling,* is an unfortunately named feature that aims to bypass the process of physically adjusting your platform to achieve this. It has nothing to do with leveling, and most printers will work perfectly well on a slight incline, or even turned upside-down, as long as the movement of the axes is parallel to the build platform.

When the required adjustment is done mechanically, it is called *tramming* (a term borrowed from CNC machining), though it is also common to see the term *leveling* used erroneously for this purpose. Trying to use tools that would normally be used for leveling for this purpose will cause endless frustration, and the term *paralleling* has been proposed to avoid confusion with leveling while having a more obvious meaning than tramming.

Rather than adjusting the platform to be parallel to the machine's axes of movement, Automatic Print Leveling adjusts the coordinate system of the print to make the axes parallel to the platform. So if your platform is tilted, your print will be tilted to match. Some printers include sensors that are used to probe the height of the platform, and these perform auto-leveling internally, so they do not need this MatterControl feature. For printers that do not have sensors for auto-leveling, MatterControl is able to perform this compensation before sending G-code to the printer.

EEPROM Settings

EEPROM stands for *Electronically Erasable Programmable Read-Only Memory.* This is a small area of memory within the microcontroller that can be used by the firmware to store variables that will not be lost when power is removed. On 3D printers, EEPROM is used to store values that may need to change if hardware is upgraded, but that you are unlikely to need to change otherwise. In other words, leave it alone unless you know what you are doing.

Gcode Terminal

Chapter 6 covers G-code, the detailed commands that actually run on your printer. Clicking the Show Terminal button opens up a window that allows you to see the commands as they execute on the printer, and, for expert users, to type in individual commands and send them to your printer. This can be useful to do things like just heat the extruder so that you can get filament into or out of it, or to move the print head if it got stuck in something.

Cloud Settings

Chapter 9 explores MatterControl's cloud capabilities in detail. Briefly, you can sign up for the cloud service, which allows you to monitor a print in progress from the web and also transfer files between your desktop computer and MatterControl Touch tablet.

Cloud Monitoring

To sign up for a cloud account, click ENABLE (when you are connected to the Internet on the device running MatterControl) and follow the online instructions to create an account.

Notification Settings

These settings allow you to select what MatterControl does when a print is finished.

Application Settings

These settings control some of the inner workings of MatterControl. We describe each one in turn here.

Update Notification Feed

This option allows you to get one of three levels of update for MatterControl: the *stable* one (the normal production version), the *beta* one (test users), or the *alpha* one (for fearless experts who do not mind being one of the first to try something). Unless you are an expert or know you need a feature not in the stable build, stick to the stable selection for now.

Language Options

These options allow you to decide which of several available languages will be used in your version.

Slice Engine

Slicing, the process of converting a 3D model into commands that can be executed on the printer is referred to as *slicing,* is described in detail in Chapter 5. As a default choice, select MatterSlice for now (which also is only option available for the tablet version).

Change Display Mode

This allows you to select Normal (computer screen) views in Matter Control, or the Touchscreen mode (with the MatterControl tablet).

Clear Print History

This clears the list of completed prints that you would otherwise get under HISTORY, on the page that displays the queue. (For more on file management, see Chapter 9.)

Theme/Display Options

This option allows you to select the background and accent colors for MatterControl screens. The top row is for the light background (used in this book's screenshots for clarity), and the bottom row is for the dark background.

The MatterControl Touch Tablet

The MatterControl Touch tablet (pictured back in Figure 2-7) comes with MatterControl already loaded. It also is wifi-capable, which is how you will get files onto it. When you have signed into MatterControl on both a desktop or laptop computer and on the MatterControl tablet, you will be able to send files to the tablet from the desktop version of MatterControl. Chapter 9 has more details on tablet operations and cloud options.

▒ **Tip**　Because MatterControl is open source software, MatterHackers maintains a *wiki* (user-supplied helpful instructions) and user forums where you may get help with any issues you may face. The wiki can be found at `http://wiki.mattercontrol.com`, and MatterHackers' forums can be found at `www.matterhackers.com/community/forum`. The MatterControl website (`www.mattercontrol.com`) has a lot of material and examples of using the software.

Summary

This chapter reviewed the basics of downloading and setting up the MatterControl software. The following chapters discuss how the software fits into the 3D-printing workflow and how to use it to create prints.

PART II

■ ■ ■

The 3D-Printing Process

This part covers the nuts and bolts of the 3D-printing workflow. To create a 3D print, first you need to make or otherwise acquire (through downloading or scanning) a 3D model of an object; we cover this in Chapter 4.

Then the model has to be sliced into layers, and those layers need to be turned into commands for a print head to follow. Chapter 5 covers the slicing process and its many options, and Chapter 6 goes over how to control your printer. Both these chapters clarify how MatterControl fits into this process.

Chapter 7 goes into the material choices you will make when you print, discussing the various types of filament that a desktop 3D printer can use.

Finally, Chapter 8 covers special cases, like hollow prints, vases, and printers that have the ability to print in multiple materials.

CHAPTER 4

■ ■ ■

Making a 3D Model

Once you have downloaded, installed, and configured MatterControl, your next step in using a 3D printer will be to find or create a 3D computer model. MatterControl has fairly limited ability to do this itself (see Chapter 11's discussion of plugins), but fortunately there are lots of programs out there, many of which are free. Depending on your needs, you may want to start simple (this chapter describes some options) or you may be entering the field as an animator or engineer who is an expert modeler already. We try to touch on some of the differences between modeling for display on a screen and creating something that will exist in the real world subject to gravity and other similarly inconvenient things!

3D-printable models can be obtained in various ways: by scanning an existing object, by downloading a model from the web, or by creating a model yourself. In each case, you have a lot of options to choose from. There is more to design than picking a software package, though, and there are design decisions you can make that can simplify the printing process later on.

Chapter 2 covers the basic input file requirements for MatterControl. This chapter talks about how you can get those STL or AMF files by scanning, downloading, or creating the models from scratch. For those who choose the last option, this chapter looks at 3D computer-aided design (CAD) and CAD-related programs that you can use to make a 3D model. By the end of the chapter, one way or another you should know how you can have a computer model that is ready to go on to the next stage of processing.

Where to Get 3D Models

Models can be made from scratch using a 3D-modeling program. However, if starting from zero seems daunting, you might consider scanning a model or downloading a pre-existing model from a database. Once you have it, you can print it as is or modify it in one of the design programs we discuss. Regardless of the source of the model, the file has to be in a format usable by the MatterControl *slice engines*, which convert the model into commands for the 3D printing, as you will see in Chapter 5. As discussed in Chapter 2, those formats are STL and AMF.

Scanning a Model

One way to get a model of something that already exists is to 3D scan it. Scanners at the consumer level are still a bit too complex to use easily. Most of them, in one way or another, scan a large number of images of an object from many angles and create a *point cloud* representing the object. The images have to be taken in a particular way to be able to re-create the third dimension of the image.

A point cloud is what it sounds like: a large number of unconnected points that represent the shape of the object to some degree of precision. Low-cost scanners capture images from many angles to generate this point cloud using smartphone or video game cameras. Then, either the user has to manually stitch together the point clouds or the software does it. More expensive systems use lasers to illuminate the object and create the point cloud.

Stray reflections, interference from objects in the background, and internal or concave surface features are challenging for the current crop of low-cost scanners. Resolution is a tricky thing to define accurately in these circumstances. Selection of a scanner for a given application will depend on the need for speed of capture, the accuracy required, the amount of time that can be devoted to manual cleanup, and the types of materials being scanned. Shiny and floppy things pose particular challenges.

After the stray reflections and other artifacts are removed, a scanner's software will create triangles covering the surface of the point cloud. This generates a model of the surface in the form of an STL or other file format. This process is typically referred to as creating a *mesh,* or *meshing.* For a complex model, meshing can take a very long time. Typically, the output of a scan needs some cleanup, as mentioned, to make it watertight and manifold.

Consumer-Level 3D Scanners

If you are considering purchasing a scanner and your budget is limited, there are a few different ways to go:

- Check out crowdfunding sites like www.kickstarter.com (search for "3d scanner") to see the latest developments as well as progress of previously funded systems.

- If you are a do-it-yourselfer, check out www.instructables.com to see some DIY scanning systems. The print back in Chapter 1 of a scan of Rich (Figure 1-1) is from one of these.

- To try using your smartphone as a scanner, download Autodesk 123D Catch at www.123dapp.com/catch.

Scanners for Biological Applications

Scientific users of 3D scanning and printing may need detailed, high-resolution information about biological structures. Medical professionals and those with access to computerized tomography (CT) scanners have been using CT scans as a starting point for 3D printing. CT scans can capture internal and complex, concave structures. CT scanners are not consumer items, but if you are a scientist or researcher, you might see whether a local hospital or research center offers scans on a fee-for-service basis. Different CT scanners can handle different densities and sizes of objects.

There are also "micro-CT" scanners with smaller beam sizes. University imaging centers and labs buy these smaller scanners for research projects, but often they're not used full-time, and facilities might provide scans on some sort of fee-for-service basis. Facilities with micro-CT scanners are not cheap, and thus neither are these scans. But if you are solving a real problem, micro-CT scanning may be a powerful way to get the information you need to create 3D models of structures of interest. CT scanners usually output a DICOM file. A web search will reveal various free and proprietary tools to convert DICOM files to STL files, depending on the specific application at hand.

▓ **Tip** The National Institutes of Health (NIH) has a site for sharing of methodologies and results using 3D printing (http://3dprint.nih.gov). This site says that in time it will be a repository of tools and tutorials for setting up various biology-oriented workflows, so be sure to check it now and again for new capability.

Downloading and Modifying Existing Models

Sometimes a model of something that you would like to print already exists. In that case, you may be able to download it from one of a growing number of model databases. Some databases contain fun items and household objects. Some of the existing models in databases are of complex, specialized objects that might be very useful to you professionally.

Many databases of 3D-printable objects are available online. The Thingiverse (`www.thingiverse.com`) and Youmagine (`www.youmagine.com`) websites both feature a wide range of objects, from sci-fi figurines to parts for enhancing 3D printers. These models have been contributed by users and as such vary widely in the quality of their design both for printing and for their intended purposes.

▦ **Note**   Sometimes model creators will upload both the STL file for printing and the file in the original format of the software that created the model. That means if you happen to be conversant in the original program, you can start with an object and modify it. For example, in Thingiverse, when you click the Download This Thing! button, you get both a list of the available files and the type of license under which it is being made available. Sometimes the developer just wants you to credit them if you use it. Sometimes commercial use is not allowed. If you obtain something from one of these databases, be sure to look carefully at the requirements, particularly if you are going to modify the object or sell something based on it.

The Instructables website (`www.instructables.com`) often includes instructions for the entire workflow to create and print a 3D model. Although not a 3D model specific site, Instructables is a good place to start because many models include fabrication instructions in addition to an STL file. Sometimes the instructions even extend to how to use the object. Instructables is a community website with all content contributed by its users. As of mid-2015, the site stated that it had over 100,000 different sets of instructions covering everything from cooking to lab equipment.

Just as there are stock image sites where you can buy the rights to 2D images, there is now a market for stock 3D models, including Flat Pyramid (`www.flatpyramid.com`) and TurboSquid (`www.turbosquid.com`). At the moment the models on these sites are more oriented to the animation and virtual reality industries. You will need to exercise some care in buying a 3D-printable model (looking for one in STL format is a first step), but as these sites become more aware of the 3D-printing consumer market, there will likely be more of them.

There is now a search engine that looks at other 3D-printing model sites: `www.yeggi.com`. You can use this site to see if there is a free or for-purchase 3D-printable file available somewhere. This site aggregates from a lot of other sites, so the cautions noted earlier apply.

If you want to modify a file that you have downloaded beyond scaling it bigger or smaller, you will need to import it into one of the programs described in the next section and essentially make a new model based on the one you have. Depending on the power of the program you use, you may be a bit limited in what sorts of things you can change.

▦ **Caution**   Do not assume that an STL file you download from a site is perfect or that it will work on your printer. On download sites that allow comments or that have an "I made one!" contribution area, see whether anyone besides the author *has* made one. If not, that might be a bad sign. If in doubt, you can run files through MeshLab (see Tip in Chapter 2) or a similar program to see if they have errors. Also be careful about scaling objects up or down—you may wind up with features that are too small to print (typically, about 1 mm is a minimum feature size—a lot bigger if the feature is embedded in support material).

Creating a 3D Model from Scratch

If you want to print something that does not exist anywhere, you will need to use software yourself to develop a new model. Fortunately, many software packages are available that make developing particular types of models as simple as possible. The next section helps you think about what software package you might want to learn about, if you do not already use one.

Using a 3D-Modeling Program

Most 3D-modeling programs will either save a file as STL or OBJ directly or offer an option to "export to" STL. Which program is the right one for the job? This section describes commonly used programs that range in price from open source and/or free to quite expensive. The programs also vary in the steepness of their learning curves. In general, the more powerful the program, the longer it takes to be reasonably proficient in its use.

Some programs have the user write computer-code–like instructions, whereas others require a lot of mouse use and more of an artistic bent. This is a quick overview of the available options; for the most part, the open source programs offer extensive documentation available for free download. The proprietary software programs typically offer training or have help available.

The descriptions here assume that the development of a model is separate from the preparation of that model for 3D printing in a slicing program. Some 3D-printer companies are beginning to develop integrated programs that combine all these steps; those programs are beyond the scope of this book. Most of these proprietary integrated systems also allow importing STL files created by other programs or from databases.

Types of 3D-Modeling Software

Table 4-1 lists some common types of 3D-modeling software. Each category represents one particular way of representing the 3D shape. Several of them actually have some capability to use more than one of these methods or may even blend these approaches, but we've tried to place each in the most appropriate category.

Table 4-1. *Types of 3D-Modeling Software*

Type of Model	Examples
Voxel	3D Coat, Minecraft
Constructive Solid Geometry (CSG)	OpenSCAD, TinkerCAD
Mesh/Non-Uniform Rational B-Splines (NURBS)	Blender, Maya, Rhinoceros 3D, 3ds Max
Feature-based parametric modeling	FreeCAD, Autodesk Inventor, SolidWorks, Solid Edge
Digital sculpting	Zbrush, Meshmixer, Leopoly, Sculptris

For example, one way of representing a 3D shape that some modeling programs use is in *voxels*. A 2D image meant to be displayed on a screen is broken up into tiny squares called pixels, each of which is a single color. When you extend this approach to three dimensions, you get voxels (*volume* + *pixel*). A 3D space is divided up into these tiny cubes, each one representing either a material or empty space, and the overall shape makes up an object. Some games, notably Minecraft, use this approach, but it is otherwise pretty uncommon.

The more common approach is to define the surface of an object, the boundary between the inside and the outside. Many 3D-modeling programs, especially those designed for 3D graphics for games or movies, let you alter the 2D polygons that make up this 3D surface, known as a *mesh*. Mesh editors may work directly on the points where multiple polygons converge, but most also offer higher-level tools that allow you to modify many points at once. One way to do this is by using Non-Uniform Rational B-Splines (NURBS) to create a smooth surface out of relatively few control points by mathematically interpolating the space between them. A problem with mesh-based editors is that they are only trying to represent surfaces, and they don't care if there are holes in the surface (places where there is no separation between the inside and outside) or self-intersections (places where the surface crosses itself). These models may look fine on the screen, which is all these programs are intended to accomplish, but they can become big problems when you try to 3D print your creation (objects that have these types of problems are called *non-manifold*). Some programs use a similar but more abstract method called *digital sculpting*. In these programs, you generally start with a plain sphere and then use tools with names like "push," "pull," and "pinch" to work the surface like clay into the desired shape, and if this is all that you do to your object, it should remain manifold.

CAD programs, on the other hand, are specifically designed to only represent shapes that can physically exist. One way to do this is by using a method known as Constructive Solid Geometry (CSG). In CSG, you start with solid objects—usually primitives like cuboids, spheroids, and cylinders—and then add and subtract them from one another to create features. If you want a block with a round hole though it, you create the block without the hole, then create a cylinder representing the hole, and then subtract the cylinder from the block.

Another approach common among CAD programs is *feature-based parametric modeling*. In this method, you generally start with a 2D drawing of one side of an object, including what all the features look like from that side. You add dimensions and relations to specify where those features belong in relation to one another and then either extrude that 2D drawing into three-dimensional features or map it to the surface of an existing 3D primitive. Some features are added after this, such as modifying the newly created edges with *fillets* or *chamfers* (two types of rounded edges), but most of the editing is done in the 2D drawings.

We have picked out a few to discuss in this chapter, primarily programs that are free or in very common professional use. With the boom in 3D printing, many new programs have entered the market, and longtime players have added offerings; if you outgrow some of the simple programs here, you might inquire at a local hackerspace or makerspace about the next logical step up for your particular need. Autodesk has a pretty full suite of tools for 3D applications and might be a good place to browse (`www.autodesk.com`) starting with the free Tinkercad, about which more in a moment.

▓ **Caution**   Some software packages are geared toward creating models meant to be viewed on a computer or theater screen (called *3D rendering*). A "3D" movie normally does not contain the parts of the model that you do not see on the screen at that moment. Various tricks exploit the way your eyes perceive 3D and fool you into thinking you are seeing a 3D image when really all you are seeing is two versions of a 2D image from slightly different perspectives. If you are at a 3D movie looking at a 3D stereo image of the north side of a tree, that side was generated in a computer. The south side of the tree, the underside of the trunk, and some of the top, east, and west sides are not needed for the movie viewer to see the tree in 3D. However, all of that *would be* needed to print the tree. Be sure the software you are looking into can export an STL file or a format that can be converted into STL.

Options for Getting Started Quickly

If you want to go from "zero to plastic" as soon as possible, you might try Tinkercad (`www.tinkercad.com`) and OpenSCAD (`www.openscad.org`), both of which are free. Tinkercad requires registration; OpenSCAD is open source. Both have example files available that you can play with and use as guidelines for your own first project.

Tinkercad: Drag and Drop

If you want to use something simple that requires no programming knowledge at all, you will like Tinkercad. Tinkercad is a member of Autodesk's suite of 3D-printing productivity tools. The program is free as of this writing, although it requires the user to register. Tinkercad is a purely drag-and-drop program that supplies a lot of simple shapes such as rectangular solids, spheres, cylinders, three-dimensional letters of the alphabet, numbers, and so on. Printable objects are created by assembling them out of these standard virtual pieces.

Tinkercad requires a good Internet connection because the program is entirely cloud-based and frequently saves incrementally. If several people are using it on one wifi node, the results can be frozen screens and frustration. However, it is a great way to develop something quickly just to test the end-to-end process of creating a model, slicing it, and printing it.

Tinkercad has extensive tutorials that are arranged into bite-sized brief walkthroughs of the key features, and there are a lot of examples that others have designed and put out there for you to play with and build upon. The classic project to try first on a 3D printer is a small keychain fob decorated with 3D initials or a few hearts. Most people can do a project of that scale in an hour or so starting from zero with Tinkercad. Figure 4-1 shows a design from Tinkercad (displayed in MatterControl), and Figure 4-2 shows the resulting object.

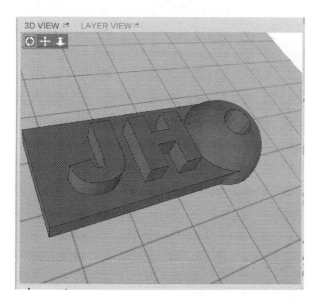

Figure 4-1. An object designed in Tinkercad and displayed in MatterControl

Figure 4-2. *The resulting 3D-printed keychain fob*

To get started in Tinkercad, do the following:

- Register as a user.

- Open one of the public models, or drag and drop basic shapes from the menus on the right.

- Shapes (say, a cube and a cylinder) can be merged by selecting them both and then click the Group Button. See the tutorials in Tinkercad for lots of ideas.

- Save your model It to STL by selecting Design ➤ Download for 3D Printing ➤ STL.

- You should now have an STL file in your downloads folder that you can import into MatterControl, slice (see Chapter 5 for more), and ultimately print.

Alternatively, you can take one of the public Tinkercad models and alter it a bit, if the model creator allows that, and then save it to STL. If you are more ambitious, sketch out something you want to build. Remember to start small and simple—see the discussions in later chapters to see what makes a model "simple." Try some of the tutorials available on the Tinkercad site in the "Learn" section and then give it a shot.

Be sure to save the object before you log out. By default, Tinkercad names things in a strange pidgin-Swedish way; you can change that by going to Design ➤ Properties and then giving it a new name. You can also change the default license for others in that same area.

OpenSCAD: A CAD Programming Environment

OpenSCAD follows the opposite philosophy from Tinkercad in that it is not drag and drop at all, and the only mouse interaction is for adjusting how you view the model you have developed. OpenSCAD uses a programming language very similar to C to define geometrical shapes, translations, rotations, and so on. The program has built-in functions for most common shapes, although the names can be a little misleading. For example, cuboids are referred to simply as "cubes," even if the lengths of their sides are not equal. Quite complex shapes can be built up easily. Figures 4-3 and 4-4 show what we will call "the spiral horn" in OpenSCAD and after it prints. We use the spiral horn in Chapter 5 to talk about support; it is a very easy piece to design in OpenSCAD, but pretty challenging to print well!

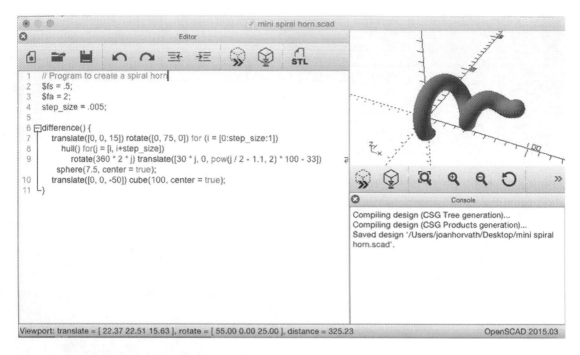

Figure 4-3. Spiral horn in OpenSCAD

Figure 4-4. OpenSCAD object 3D-printed from the code in Figure 4-3

To try out a simple model in OpenSCAD, do the following:

- Click the File menu.

- Pick an example from the Examples submenu (or click File ➤ New and then type in the little example shown in Figure 4-3 — what is shown is all you need).

- Click Design ➤ Render (if it is a complex object, you might want to Preview first).

- Assuming this still looks good, save it with File ➤ Save. This saves the program in OpenSCAD format, not STL.

- Click File ➤ Export ➤ Export as STL.

You can then take the STL file and run it through a slicing program (see Chapter 5), and you will be ready to print (see Chapter 6). OpenSCAD is particularly suited to modeling objects that can be built up out of geometric shapes. Complex objects are possible by starting with these basic shapes and rotating them. You can make impressive geometries with a little programming experience and the OpenSCAD manual.

If you want to build something simple quickly and you like writing code better than using a mouse, OpenSCAD may be for you. If you have never done any programming, though, it is probably not the best choice. Typically we suggest that beginning users try both Tinkercad and OpenSCAD, as two very different options for getting started, and then migrate into other more sophisticated or expensive programs after getting their feet wet.

Programs for Specific Applications

Tinkercad and OpenSCAD are great for beginners. If you are using your printer mostly as a hobbyist, in a classroom, or to make fun objects around the house, you can probably be happy for a long time with these programs. However, if you need to create professional-level sculptural models, or if you need dimensioned drawings (drawings meant to be read by a person with numbers for dimensions, angles and so on printed on them), then these programs probably are not enough. Many, many design programs can either produce an STL file or a file that can be translated into STL. Most of these programs deserve (and in some cases have) their own book-length tutorials.

Generally speaking, you need to consider a few key attributes when selecting a design program. First, consider your own strengths: are you good at programming, or are you better at using a mouse? Do you have decent hand-eye coordination and drawing skills? How much time do you have to devote to becoming proficient, and how much design are you really going to do? A program with a short learning curve but limited capability might be okay if you are only going to make a few complicated objects, but learning a more-capable program may be worth it if those extra features will vastly enhance your productivity.

Some software only runs on either Mac or Windows, not both. If you only have access to one or the other operating system, that may force a choice. Functionality can be different between Mac and Windows versions of a particular package, particularly in the open source world.

Next, consider budget. Free and open source software varies in its quality; documentation can be uneven or incomplete for open source software. However, it *is* free. For pricey software, research whether demonstration versions of the software are available and, if so, try before you buy. If you are a student, check with your school or the software publisher to see whether any discounts are available to you.

With all that said, programs to create models for 3D printing need to serve two broad categories of users. Engineers, architects, industrial designers, mathematicians, and similar professionals need to create 2D drawings with labeled, numerical dimensions and great precision so that teams of people can make things together. Often they need to integrate 3D-printed parts with traditionally manufactured ones and thus will need both the ability to create a file for printing and a traditionally dimensioned, human-readable drawing. Artists may want good drawing tools that allow them to sketch freely but not require as much precision. Different tools have evolved for these respective communities, as we will see next.

Engineering and Architecture Programs

Engineers, industrial designers, and architects use 3D-modeling programs oriented toward applications that require precision. The open source program FreeCAD (`www.freecadweb.org`) is a parametric modeling engineering-oriented program with many features that used to be available only in very expensive programs. FreeCAD runs on Mac, Windows, and Linux machines.

A common (but expensive) engineering tool is the Solidworks program from Dassault Systèmes. Solidworks is designed to create real engineering projects and as such is a good end-to-end program to go from concept to final dimensioned parts. It does take a while to become proficient in Solidworks, however, and cost can be a barrier. Solidworks is only available for Windows.

Google's Sketchup program is focused on making it easy to lay out an architectural project, including a large library of many common home fixtures from various manufacturers. Sketchup can be used more broadly, but it focuses mostly on assembling geometrical and precise models, and the resulting models may require format conversion and have problems with 3D printing (Sketchup is notorious for creating non-manifold models).

Mathematica (`www.wolfram.com/mathematica/`) is a programming system that allows users to model complicated mathematical functions. Mathematica creates STL files based on user-generated mathematical models. That means it is possible to develop sophisticated mathematical models and then visualize them in physical form. This possibility has many implications, particularly for people who teach courses that use Mathematica. A natural spectrum of mathematics visualization options starts with OpenSCAD and moves up to Mathematica.

Visual-Effects and Sculptural Programs

Visual-effects developers, animators, and similar artists develop 3D models in computer programs that are good for complex, curved, organic objects such as characters in animated films. Most of these either can export an STL file directly or employ translation utilities and procedures to take their output and turn it into STL. The commercial program Rhino, for example, exports directly into STL.

The Maya animation program (`www.autodesk.com/products/maya`) exports OBJ files, which MatterControl can read once you translate them to STL. However, Maya is a mesh-based modeler. That means that when you draw something, you are creating an infinitely thin "mesh" that defines the surface. For example, if you model a ball and cut it in half, you are creating a cup-shaped thing with zero thickness. The software later in the 3D-printing workflow will do unpredictable things with this. You need to use the extrude functions of the modeling software to give your mesh some thickness. Once you are sure your mesh has finite thickness everywhere, you can safely export it as an OBJ file. As of this writing, Maya comes with a plugin that generates OBJ files, but the plugin by default is not enabled. Use Maya's Plugin Manager to enable the OBJexport plugin so you can then export Maya's native format to OBJ files.

If budget is an issue, Blender is an open source visual-effects development program, available from `www.blender.org`. Like many 3D graphics programs, Blender can export to STL format. It is extremely powerful—you can make an entire animated film with it—but has a correspondingly steep learning curve. If you are very fast with a mouse, this may be the program for you, but the program is notorious for "thinking" differently from all other programs.

▓ **Caution** Because programs like Maya or Blender are intended only for creating models that will look right when rendered as 2D images, the user has to do some extra work to ensure that the models that it produces will be manifold. You will have to make sure that your meshes are all closed and have no unnecessary internal geometry or self-intersections, or your slicing program and printer might both do unpredictable things. If you want to turn a 2D surface into a printable mesh, you will need to extrude or "solidify" it so that it has a thickness of at least a millimeter or two. Be sure you are working in millimeters first or you might make inch- or centimeter-thick walls!

Zbrush (`www.zbrush.com`) is another commercial program for artists. It is a complex but very capable program that allows the user to sculpt in virtual clay. Users often abandon the mouse and draw instead on a tablet with a stylus to create very sophisticated, realistic designs of animated characters and the like.

Design Considerations

Chapter 5 covers the details you need to think about when preparing a 3D printer model for upload onto a printer. But before getting into that, let's take a step back and ask why use a 3D printer at all? What are some of the big advantages, and how can you avoid "fighting the printer" (asking it to do things it is just not meant to do)? And on the flip side, when is it a bad idea to use a 3D printer?

Complexity Is Free (but Simplicity May Not Be)

One of the mantras of the 3D-printer community is that *complexity is free*. Because 3D-printed parts are built up one layer at a time, it really does not matter whether that layer is one unbroken sheet or an intricate design. Consumer-level printers have one more strong advantage: the opportunity to iteratively design something, see how it came out, and then change the design if necessary. When that became possible in in the 1980s for computing in general (versus overnight batch jobs), there was a fundamental change to the process of creating software.

We all hope the same thing is about to happen for making physical things. Business models based on the ability to rapidly iterate hardware design are starting to be called *hardware as a service* (an analogy to *software as a service*). How these business models will play out in the marketplace remains to be seen. With that said, though, sometimes a print that looks simple actually is challenging to print. We talk about this some in Chapter 5 and 6, and show some examples in Chapters 8 and 10. Experience and knowing some design rules (given in Chapter 5) must be your guide.

Speed vs. Customization

The counterargument to *complexity is free* is that complexity may matter less in 3D printing than in conventional fabrication, but complex prints may take a long time. Consumer 3D printers take a while to print anything out—it is rare for a print of any size to take less than a few hours, and prints that take a day are routine.

If you are making one of something or a prototype for a mold, such a length of time may be competitive with that of a machinist or other professional making a prototype in a way that involves a lot of labor. But if the part is simple or you want a lot of them, a 3D-printed part is probably not the way to go. If you are happily creating injection-molded parts for something now, then a 3D-printed part is *definitely* not the way to go.

To narrow it down a bit more, consumer 3D printers may not be the best fit for your project if everything you do will require a lot of hand-finishing after the fact. You might consider using a service bureau to do one of the more industrial processes. To put it another way, only the right kind of complexity is free.

3D printing has a role in creating items that are by their nature one-of-a-kind (or a-few-of-a-kind) and that work well with the technology. Time will tell what the best applications are. Our sense is that one key role for 3D printing is that it makes the front of the product-development process faster. People who would have made a computer model and then created a foam-core physical mockup as two separate chores are obviously better off with a 3D printer.

Other promising markets exist in industries that make custom parts for one-of-a-kind applications (or, even better, industries that *should* operate that way but cannot do so economically at the moment). The biggest market now, though, is a somewhat intangible one: allowing people to make stuff again just because they want to and can. With the ready availability of small and midsized 3D printers, manufacturing may become more and more distributed—when you buy something, you may get a file to print your purchase, rather than having a piece of plastic created elsewhere and flown to you. The long-term business implications of this are just beginning to become apparent.

Summary

In this chapter you learned about the beginning of the 3D-printing process. The first step is creating or finding a 3D digital model of your object, which requires you to visit a website with objects available for download, 3D-scan something that already exists, or learn one of the many available 3D-modeling software packages. The chapter went over the various types of software packages available for the engineer versus the artist to generate a standard (STL) 3D-printing file. Chapter 5 takes that STL file through the next steps.

■ ■ ■

Slicing a 3D Model

This chapter and the next are the core of this book's explanation of the 3D-printing process. 3D printers cannot use a computer model until that model is changed into commands to move around an extruder (see Chapter 1) and control when that extruder is and is not putting down material. Because the types of 3D printers controlled by MatterControl lay up a layer at a time of some material, the first part of the software workflow (described in this chapter) cuts the model into layers, normally referred to as *slicing*. 3D printing is easier than machining, but a lot harder than (2D) consumer printing. We have found cooking to be an apt metaphor, and will expand on that shortly.

The first part of this chapter teaches you about the best ways to design a model so that it prints easily, which we call *3D-printing design rules*. We also try to give you some background about why these rules work.

Then we move on to the specifics of how MatterControl has implemented slicing at three levels of sophistication. If you are an absolute beginner, you can use the Simple settings, then move on to Intermediate, and then to Advanced. With the current state of the art, damaging open source 3D printers is all too possible if you use inappropriate slicing settings that crash parts into each other, try to force too much filament through the nozzle, or commit similar sins.

This is because most open source 3D printers are *open loop* robots to a greater or lesser degree. An open loop system does not use any *feedback* (information from sensors) to see how it is performing. The implication of this is that these 3D printers that do not check whether a command they have been given will put the printer in a state that will physically damage it. Different printers check different things (they usually control temperature with a feedback mechanism and usually have *end stops* that tell the machine that the print head has gone as far as it can go), but often that's about it. For the rest, the user needs to know how to keep the printer within bounds. This design strategy makes them cheap and simple, but vulnerable to bad commands.

This chapter gives you background to do everything from a first print to a major project. Chapter 8 talks about some special cases, such as printers that have the ability to print in multiple materials at once, and objects that are hollow (like a vase). Chapter 10 has several example projects to bring it all together, including some classic beginner ones to get you started.

What Is "Slicing"?

Creating an STL file (described in Chapter 4) is the first part of the 3D-printing process. The next step, and the focus of this chapter, is to divide, or *slice,* the file into layers that the printer can generate. The slicing program has to take into account both the physical characteristics of the printer and the geometry of the model being printed. The final step is to make a G-code file (commands to drive the printer), which we will get to in Chapter 6.

You would not expect an oven to have one big button that simply said, BAKE. Similarly, the state of the art in consumer 3D printing is such that you need to be comfortable determining a number of different settings, like things you deal with in a recipe: materials, temperature, how fast you will push plastic out of the nozzle, and so on. The virtue of an open source printer is that, like a master chef, you can tweak your printer settings to get fantastic results. The downside is that you need to be at least a little bit of a cook to get results.

3D Printing as Cooking

Imagine you want to bake a cake. First, you might decide in general what kind of cake you want to make. You will either page around in a cookbook for ideas or create something new from your imagination; that's like creating the STL file or finding one to download from the web, as you did in Chapter 4.

Then you would get a detailed recipe for the ingredients, determine the temperature and length of time you will bake the cake, mix up the ingredients, and pour them into a pan. These actions require some experience with cooking, such as understanding what it means to *grease* and *flour* a *cake pan.* Knowing your oven, you might set the temperature a little differently than the recipe says or change things around to make cupcakes or to make the recipe work if you live at high altitude. This part of the process is the equivalent of slicing in 3D printing: taking your creation and figuring out what material to use, how the tools you will use will actually interact with the ingredients, and handling similar "real world" issues.

Finally, you would put the cake in the oven. You would rely on the oven controls to keep the temperature where you set it and the timer to ding at the correct time. Setting the temperature and time for baking and putting the cake in the oven are the equivalent of sending the G-code to the printer.

When the cake is done, it might get a little messed up when you take out of the pan, and you may want to add icing or do something else to it before serving. The equivalent for a 3D printer is *post-processing.* Chapter 12 described various things you can do after the print comes off the platform.

You could embark on making a ten-layer cake with an elaborate icing design for your next party. However, if all you have is one beat-up layer cake pan or if you have never cooked anything before, you may not get there, at least not on your first try. Similarly, you need to have a realistic idea about what types of objects you can make with your printer at your current level of sophistication and work up to grander things.

Chapter 3 suggests how to set up MatterControl for your machine, which would create default slicing settings. Start with those, use the information in this chapter to understand what those settings are doing, and take the next steps when those defaults are no longer enough. Be aware, though, that most open source printers have limited or no ability to stop you if you send commands that will print a pile of string instead of the desired object. The printer also may not recognize that it is having a mechanical problem. Just as you would while cooking on an unfamiliar stove with a new recipe, be sure to keep an eye on what the printer is doing, don't leave it unattended, and think through the implications of your settings. The next section goes over your software "kitchen tools" and talks about how you can use them to realize your imagined creations.

The Physicality of 3D Printing

3D-printed objects are born as computer files, and their images on a computer screen can be as fantastically complex as desired. A 3D model may look great on a computer screen, but additional structure may be necessary to make the model printable. It is possible to draw anything, but gravity and the mechanics of the printer can limit what is possible to print. For example, layers cannot be laid down in mid-air, and the model has to fit inside the volume the specific printer has available for printing. The model is just a surface—an infinitely thin layer between the inside and outside of the designed object—and you need to make a lot of decisions about how that will be translated into a physical object.

If you have ever printed something on a regular 2D paper printer and been frustrated that only half the page printed out or that the print had purple lines across it, you can probably imagine that the equivalent types of problems become more varied and subtler to debug when working in 3D. To avoid these problems, various techniques have been developed. We introduce those here and then show you how to access them in MatterControl as we go.

Before anything else matters, the model has to stick to the platform so that it can be built up layer by layer. It has to stick solidly—not peel up at the corners as it cools, and not get knocked off as subsequent layers are built on top of the first layer. Slicing software also takes into account a particular printer's platform, including how big it is, whether it is heated or not, and what type of material or covering is on the surface of the platform. Starting a print solidly is critical. Typically, a print starts with a *skirt* (a few layers printed to prime the nozzle and detect problems). Then a print might use a *brim* (some extra material around the contact points between the print and the platform) or a *raft* (a few layers under a print) to create a solid base. A heated platform and/or tape covering the platform help with adhesion, too.

Next, consider how the model will be oriented when it prints out. If the model has pieces that would require printing in mid-air (known as *overhangs*), some type of *support* has to be laid down and/or the printer has to bridge across gaps. Or perhaps the model can be printed out with a different orientation that requires less (or no) support but which introduces other design issues, such as the need to glue two halves together.

In addition to support that will be broken away, internal voids in prints have to be filled in somehow. *Infill* is a complex topic we talk about in detail later in the chapter. 3D prints are rarely solid because it takes too long and uses too much filament. Infill and support create the structure for the surface of an object as it builds up, and we talk about how all these interact later in this chapter.

3D Printing Design Rules

Engineers and designers often use *design rules*—simple things to keep in mind when creating something. Often you can break these rules, but the result may not work out as well or be more difficult to achieve. In the case of designing something to 3D print and then creating a file to be printed, the printer's design, the properties of the material, and the model geometry all affect what settings you use in the slicing programs in one way or another. The things you need to keep in mind can be summarized in the following set of design rules for the geometry of each 3D-printed part:

- Minimize overhangs—or make any overhang gradual (jutting out at a 45-degree angle or less). Overhangs at less than a 45-degree angle, or sometimes a bit steeper, usually can be printed without support.

- If you must have overhangs, try to avoid creating *caves*, which will be filled with support.

- Try to have as large a base as possible touching the platform. If only a few spots will touch, you may need to use a raft or brim (discussed later in this chapter).

- Avoid very thin features (features less than about four times the nozzle diameter —maybe 2 mm or so). In particular, avoid tall, slender structures under a few millimeters in diameter or fine structures that need support (the structure may break off before the support does). Because the positioning accuracy is much finer than the nozzle itself, the printer can produce details smaller than this, as long as they do not include features that are less than about twice the nozzle diameter in thickness.

- If you have two parts that fit together, allow clearances of about half a millimeter to one millimeter or so. Do not create a 10 mm diameter rod to fit into a 10 mm diameter hole, because it will not fit. Create an 8 or 9 mm rod instead. Later in this chapter we talk about tolerances and layer heights and go into these issues in more depth.

- Prints are stronger in the plane of the platform (*x-y* plane) because layer-to-layer adhesion is not as good as the structure within a layer. Consider this if the part will be stressed, particularly under tension.

- Prints will have layer lines. If there is an aesthetic issue with this, you may need to plan on post-processing of some kind (sanding, painting, and so on), which may introduce other constraints on which material you use for the print. Chapter 12 discusses this in depth.

- All filament-based, 3D-printable materials have fairly low melting temperatures by the nature of the technology. Some materials are more likely to deform in common circumstances like those encountered in a parked car on a summer day. See Chapter 7 for material choice considerations. Your printer may only support one material, so be aware of your limitation in this department when thinking about what you will make.

░ **Tip** If a part's geometry simply cannot meet the preceding design rules, consider using one of the software tools described in Chapter 4 to cut it into parts that do meet these criteria. Then glue these parts together after they are printed. We show this later in the chapter.

Slicing a Model Using MatterControl

MatterControl supports three slice engines, or *slicers*. Each engine is a computer program that has its own versions of the settings we describe generally in this section. You can choose from *Slic3r, CuraEngine,* or *MatterSlice*. Slic3r is the oldest and most feature-rich of these slicers. CuraEngine is a couple of years old and offers a number of optimizations and simplifications that make it easier to get good results. MatterSlice is a new slicer for MatterControl that is based on CuraEngine but adds some features that are missing from CuraEngine while remaining simpler than Slic3r.

Picking One of the Slice Engines

MatterControl gives you the choice of using one of three different *slice engines,* computer programs that take the STL model file and turn it into G-code to execute on the printer. Each of them has a reputation for being particularly good at different types of things, but any two experts might disagree on what those things are. (It's sort of like asking three car buffs what the best car for freeway driving might be.) Do a few experiments yourself printing a small object with all three with similar settings (the settings for each one are somewhat different) to get a feel for how these different codes interact with the detailed mechanisms of your printer. As described in Chapter 3, you can select the slice engine in the OPTIONS screen, under Application Settings ➤ Slice Engine.

Running the Program

To slice an object in MatterControl, first follow these steps to get the STL file you have created or downloaded (as described in Chapter 4). First, be sure you have a printer defined and selected (see Chapter 3).

Click the Add button. Locate an STL file you want to print from the directory listing that pops up and select it. It should show up in your print queue. Click the item in the queue and you will see a 3D view of it in the right side of the window if your window is wide enough. Or you can mouse over the item in the queue and select View to open the 3D view in a new window. Click the Edit pencil at the bottom of the new window to enter editing mode.

On the right-hand side of the resulting 3D view (shown in Figure 5-1), you will see options about how to display the object in the window (shown opened in Figure 5-1) as well as to Rotate, Scale, and Mirror it. If the model overflows the platform, scale it down using the Scale controls. If it is invisible, try scaling it up by 25.4 (it might have been in inches; MatterControl presumes millimeters).

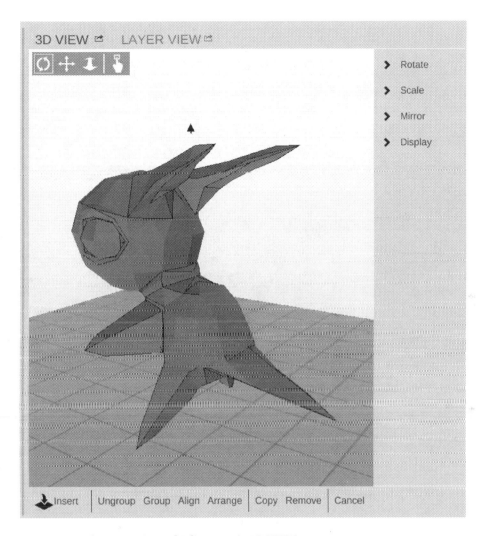

Figure 5-1. *The MatterControl Edit screen in 3D VIEW*

Will the STL file need support in its current orientation? Is there an orientation in which it would not? If so, rotate it with the Rotate controls. (The *x* and *y* axes are in the plane of the build platform; *z* is up and down.)

▒ **Tip** If an STL consists of multiple pieces and you want to move them separately, click the object and then click Ungroup at the bottom of the window. You may need to rotate each of the pieces to get them all at the best angle. Or, if the pieces are big, you may want to print them one at a time. You can click Arrange to see where the software wants to put your object.

Once you are happy with how the model piece (or collection of pieces) is oriented and scaled, the next step will be to think about whether the default settings for slicing the file are the right ones. To move to the screens that allow setting these parameters, click Settings & Controls arrow to move from the screen showing the queue (displayed back in Figure 2-2) to the screen shown in Figure 5-2. We will now walk through the two halves of that screen, with some explanatory detours along the way.

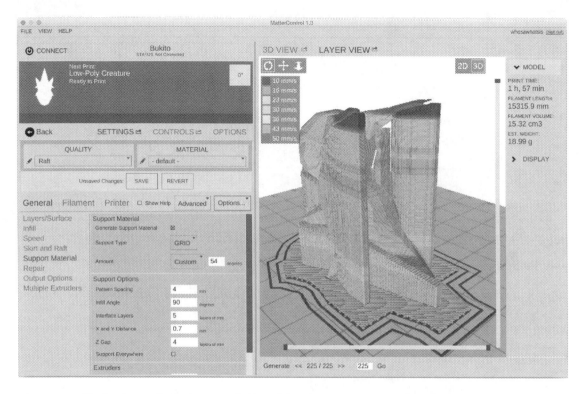

Figure 5-2. *The Settings & Controls screen (left) and the LAYER VIEW screen (right)*

Changing the Slice Engine Settings

The left side of Figure 5-2 displays the Settings & Controls view of the MatterSlice settings. There are three categories of settings: Print, Filament, and Printer. How many settings are presented to you as changeable varies with whether you choose to identify yourself as someone who wants things to be Simple, Intermediate, or Advanced.

There are two other categories of settings, though—one for Quality and one for Material. There are default values set for all of these based on the 3D printer model you selected. You can go in and change particular values of the Print, Filament, and Printer settings one at a time if you want to. But if you wanted to set up certain groups of settings to reuse over and over, you could do that with the QUALITY and MATERIAL dropdown menus. (Some settings, like Layer Height, require you to create a new entry in the QUALITY category.)

MatterControl refers to groups of settings as *pre-sets*. Let's say you wanted to change the default settings for a particular printer, which has temperatures set to print with PLA plastic, at 210 degrees C, to those for nylon, which needs to be 240 C or higher. You would go to MATERIAL, select <<ADD>>, and then walk through the options to get to extruder temperature and set it to 240. Then you would <<ADD>> any other settings you wanted to tie to nylon printing and save that set under the name Nylon. Settings in MATERIAL can come from the Print, Filament, or Printer categories, and similarly for QUALITY.

Now suppose you wanted to store a particular pre-set for models with a lot of delicate overhangs with carefully crafted support. You might create changes to those settings under QUALITY. For each print, you can thus have three overlapping pre-sets: the print/filament/printer set that comes in with the defaults for your printer (or that you set up), QUALITY, and MATERIALS. If the settings are in conflict, MATERIALS takes priority over QUALITY, which takes priority over the printer defaults.

Pre-sets are a powerful thing, because you can separate out settings you evolve for a particular material or maybe a class of objects from those that are more focused perhaps on speed of print or support versus no support. You can have as many custom items as you want in each list. Be cautious using a settings item that was developed for a different engine. Settings may be different.

You can export your pre-sets files to share with others or archive them by using the Export function when you are setting up the new pre-set (shown in Figure 5-3). Export creates a slice file that you would then import to use elsewhere. This example shows setting up a new pre-set called "0.25 layers," which sets the layer height to 0.25 mm and the infill pattern to octagramspiral.

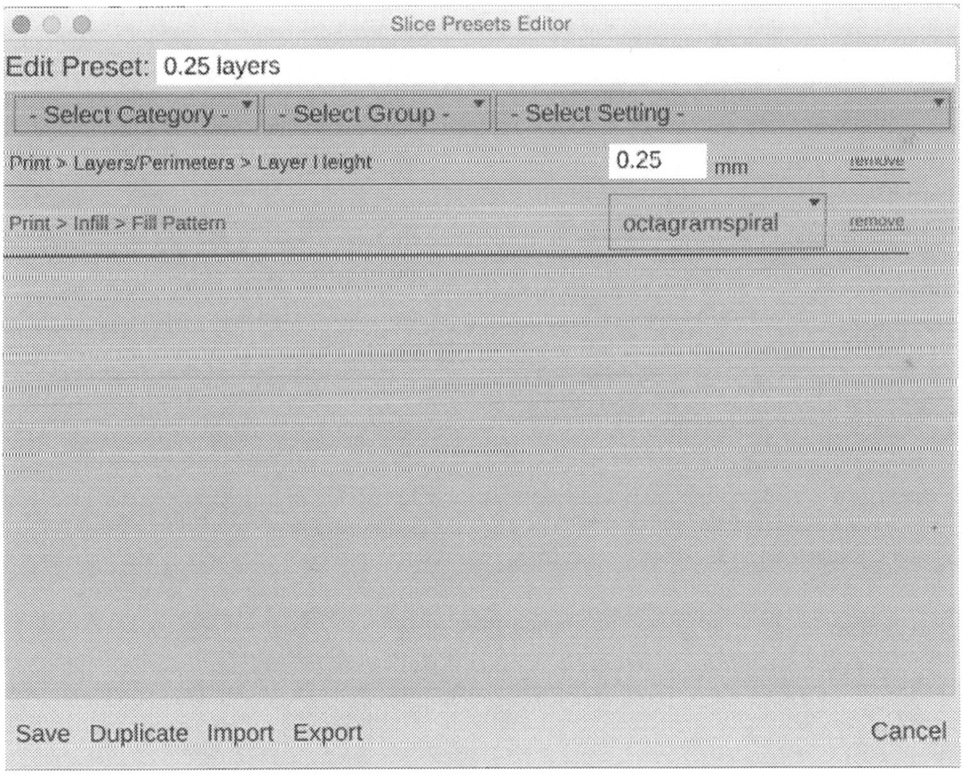

Figure 5-3. *Saving new presets*

Layer-by-Layer Preview

It takes a long time to print something on a 3D printer, so you would like to look at a simulation of how your print is going to come out before you actually get things started. MatterControl always shows you a list of the currently available parts you are working on. The left side of Figure 5-2 shows an in-depth, layer-by-layer representation of how the 3D printer will construct your object. The representation is created when you select Layer View and then when prompted select Generate. The slicing engine breaks down the object and allows you to view each layer frame by frame.

The Layer View depends on your current slicing settings and is only generated on demand. This allows you to visualize what is happening with a given print based on your current slice settings. You can see the individual lines of melted material that the software predicts your G-code will generate. In the 3D Layer View, you can select whether you want the colors that represent the speed, going from blue (slowest) to red (fastest), and select whether or not you want to see retraction (explained later in this chapter).

Saving a File to Be Printed

Once you are happy with how the print preview looks in the Layer View window from a variety of angles, it is time to print the file. Printing with a computer (or MatterControl Touch tablet) connected directly to a 3D printer is covered in Chapter 6. If you are just going to save the file to print later, click 3D VIEW to return to the view shown in Figure 5-4. Click Export ➤ Export as Gcode to save the file.

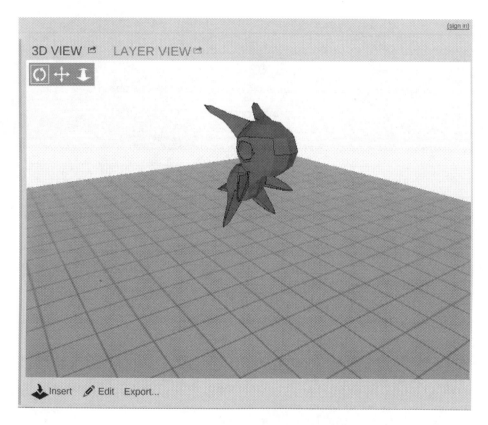

Figure 5-4. *Saving a printable file (G-code) to print later*

Slice Engine Settings and What They Mean

Now that you know how to change slice settings, what are they and what do they mean? For a quick explanation you can always tick the box that says Show Help, just above the settings. A short explanation of what every setting does appears with that setting. However, many of these settings are interrelated and need some explanation. The rest of this chapter discusses some of the commonly changed settings and their implications, and goes on a foray into print tolerances and resolution.

Starting a Print and Getting a Model to Stick to the Platform

One of the challenges with a 3D printer is getting the model to stick to the platform. Sometimes a model has a relatively small contact area with the platform, and when the extruder lays down the next layer it knocks the model loose. When that happens, the subsequent layers go in random places as the structure gets knocked around. The resulting mess is typically called *printing hair* (in polite company, anyway). There are few worse feelings than smugly demonstrating a 3D printer to your friends and then noticing that your model is being merrily dragged around the platform, trailing strands of filament. Techniques to prevent such bad hair days include using *brims* and *rafts,* and taking care to orient your model optimally on the build platform.

Skirts

A *skirt* is a few loops of filament laid down at the beginning of a print that outline all the objects being printed at a given time and show the maximum size of the first layer of the print. A skirt can solve several problems that might be encountered at the very start of a print.

It is possible to print more than one thing at a time on a 3D printer's platform. The programs for arranging the objects for a print run show you where the prints will be positioned relative to each other. However, it is always possible to create something that would wind up too big to print, since the (virtual) version can be hanging off the platform. When the skirt is drawn around all the objects that you are planning on printing, it allows you to quickly see whether there are any problems.

Also, if the color of the filament is different from that in the previous project you prined, it is good to print something away from your object first so that any material of a different color that is still in the nozzle is melted out before starting to print the main object. Generally, a skirt allows the printer to finish priming the extruder with filament before the main object starts printing.

▦ **Tip**   If the skirt falls off the edge of the platform somewhere, you can stop the print right away without wasting filament. Always watch the first few minutes of a print carefully. A skirt is not perfect insurance, though. If an upper layer is bigger and overhangs, the skirt will not show that.

The skirt is usually a few millimeters away from the location on the platform where the first layer of the main object being printed will reside. By the time a few loops are done, any previous filament should also be flushed out of the nozzle. Most programs allow the user to specify both the distance that the skirt is from the main model and the number of loops constituting the skirt.

▦ **Tip**   Add a few loops to the skirt when you change to a light-colored filament after printing a previous print with a dark filament. Doing so clears out the nozzle so there will not be any mixing of colors and resulting staining of your print. This process is described in detail in Chapter 6.

Brims

A *brim* is a first layer that is larger in extent (like a hat brim) than, strictly speaking, the object's first layer needs to be. A brim usually is specified in terms of width away from the object. A few millimeters usually make a big difference. CuraEngine and MatterSlice lack an explicit brim feature, but you can still create one by setting the skirt's distance from the object to zero so that it is touching the object.

▨ **Note**   Experts often make the first layer of a print a lot thicker than subsequent layers to be sure the print sticks. A thick layer plus a brim can make it a lot more likely a print with a small contact area will survive to the end. Although all of these slicers support both making the first layer thicker and increasing the extrusion width for the first layer, as of this writing, MatterControl's interface does now allow you to set the first layer extrusion width when using CuraEngine.

Without the ability to increase extrusion width, it is sometimes counterintuitively better to print the first layer thinner so that the ratio of width over thickness (W/T) is higher, as it is this value that has the most to do with platform adhesion. A thicker first layer with the same extrusion width will have a lower W/T ratio, which weakens adhesion, but a thinner first layer is more sensitive to platforms that are not perfectly smooth, flat, and at the perfect distance from the nozzle. This is why some users use a thicker first layer to strike a balance between adhesion strength and uneven platforms.

Rafts

When you look at the lists of settings in a slicing program you may see options for a raft. A *raft* (in the sense of the word like something a shipwreck victim would make) is a few layers of support material underneath a print. In the early days of 3D printing, when beds were often uneven and there were no heated platforms, rafts could help prints stick better. In those early days, it was often nearly impossible to completely remove the raft from the print, especially with PLA, but slicers have recently gotten much better at controlling the adhesion between the print and raft. (With MatterSlice, there is an "air gap" setting to adjust the adhesion between the print and raft). Before these improvements were added, though, the practice of using rafts had largely gone out of favor, because a good first layer and perhaps a brim are often a better combination on a modern printer.

Sometimes if something is only touching the platform in a few places and will be printed mostly on top of supports, though, a raft can be a good choice to ensure that the first layer of those support structures will be ancored to the platform. Figure 5-2 shows a skirt and raft as the software predicts it, and Figure 5-5 shows the same thing on a printer. Note that the points on the ears were a little marginal in how thick they were; very thin objects on top of support can be a little risky.

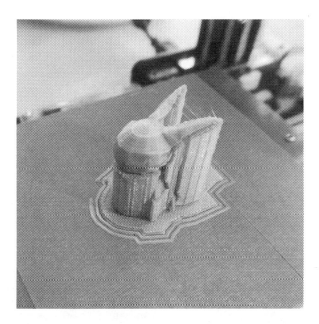

Figure 5-5. *The same object as in Figure 5-2, but now being printed; note the skirt, raft and heavy support*

Heated Platforms, Tape, and Other Sticky Stuff

Another key factor in keeping the model firmly attached to the platform is the surface of the platform itself. Depending on the model of 3D printer and the filament, there are a variety of ways to ensure that the first layer of the print does not peel off.

The first consideration is whether or not a printer has a heated platform. Some materials (such as acrylonitrile butadiene styrene, ABS) require a heated platform. (See Chapter 7 for details and Table 7-1 in particular for recommended temperatures for different materials.) Otherwise, prints will tend to contract as they cool and "warp" or "lift" up from the platform around the edges as the upper layers cool and contract while sticking to the already-cooled layers below. Heated platforms typically are covered with heat-resistant tape (such as Kapton or PET/polyester tape) that can be replaced as the surface gets a little beat up from users scraping off models. Some manufacturers suggest you print on bare glass, supply glue sticks to rub on the platform, or suggest spraying on hairspray.

Machines intended to print primarily polylactic acid (PLA) plastic do not require heated platforms. PLA can print just fine on a room-temperature platform with an appropriate surface. Consumer printers often recommend covering unheated platforms with blue painter's masking tape (in particular, 3M Scotch Blue brand) to get a good solid base for PLA models while still enabling them to be pried off reasonably easily. The tape should be put on as smoothly and evenly as possible.

▩ **Caution**   If you have an unheated platform, set the platform temperature in the slicing software to 0 degrees. Otherwise, some slicing programs may generate G-code to wait for the platform temperature to warm up to a particular temperature based on the filament material. If you do not have a platform heater, your printer will simply sit and wait for an event that will never occur.

To print PLA on a heated platform covered with Kapton tape, the platform needs to be heated somewhat to get the PLA to stick to the Kapton (see Chapter 7 for details). Some manufacturers provide a glue stick or something else to coat the platform for each print. In that case, follow the manufacturer's directions for the printer and the filament material.

▨ **Tip**   An artist's spatula or painter's knife (available at any art supply store) is a good tool for getting models off platforms. A fairly stiff one with a blade a few inches long can pry a big model off a platform while leaving delicate structures unharmed.

Supporting and Orienting a Model

Most consumer 3D printers build up their models from a platform, whether the extruder is fixed and the platform drops away or the extruder head moves up and away from a platform. This means that in some cases, a print head would be laying down material in air. For example, imagine a statue with an outstretched arm. Assuming that the statue is being printed up from its base, the initial bottom layers of the arm would print into the air and fall down unless something was printed into the open space all the way up from the platform. Material printed like this is called *support*. Sometimes this problem can be minimized or eliminated altogether by printing the model in a different orientation. This section talks about these interacting considerations.

Support

In a 3D print, the first layer sticks to the platform. Then the second layer is added above that, and so on, like a brick wall. In the case of the wall, if there are no bricks under the second layer (or at least some bricks partially lapped under it), the second layer of brick will fall to the ground.

In 3D printing, the structures that prevent the equivalent problem are called *support*. The slicing process generates support automatically in some programs, and with some user control in others. In general, it is best to avoid support if possible because removing it is time-consuming and the process of pulling it off can damage the model. You will then need to remove the support mechanically (with needle-nosed pliers, a screwdriver, and ultimately tweezers or another small tool to take off the last bits). The print in Figure 5-5 shows a small creature that needed a lot of support structure. Figure 5-6 shows another example: the spiral horn we developed back in Chapter 4's section on OpenSCAD, shown in Figures 4-3 and 4-4.

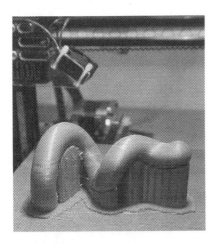

Figure 5-6. *The object from Figures 4-3 and 4-4, as it came off a printer*

Orientation

A particular model may seem to have a side that is "supposed" to be the bottom of the model. Sometimes, though, turning a model so that it lies on its side or even upside-down can increase the first-layer contact with the platform and decrease the amount of support. Particularly if you are going to be printing the object more than once, spending some time playing with the orientation of a complex model is worthwhile.

A bit of thought can sometimes also eliminate support that the slicing software would automatically create in hard-to-get-at places, like internal narrow spaces. Sometimes turning a complicated object through some arbitrary rotation—such as 10 degrees about the x axis, 15 degrees in y, and 90 in z—will result in the best situation with the least support needed.

▓ **Tip**   You can name a file in a way that reminds you of a good rotation for it. For example, butterfly_x80-y60-z25.stl is an STL file representing a butterfly that is best printed after rotating 80 degrees about the x axis, 60 about the y, and 25 about the z. Otherwise, it can be hard to keep track of the best orientation you came up with if you are going to generate related STL files repeatedly—for example, as the output of an iterative design process.

The creature in Figure 5-5 was printed so that the support was in the least-complex possible areas. However, this orientation will leave some support scars in a very visible spot. There are always tradeoffs. A bit of patience and sandpaper can minimize this scarring. Chapter 12 talks more about post-processing. That said, there is a lot of lore about how to create the most effective support that is easy to peel off. Objects printed in PLA often have some residual bits of support that can be hard to remove and that can leave scars when the last bits are pulled off. A bit of the support grid might remain stuck on the model surface and be difficult to get off. A pair of needle-nosed pliers can grab one end of the support and get a clean pull-off started, or a screwdriver can be levered under the edge of the support to try and pull it off cleanly. Strong tweezers can be used to pick off the last bits. Various slicing programs have recently started concentrating on developing better break-away support algorithms, particularly for PLA.

▒ **Tip**   Support usually comes off a model printed in ABS more readily than the same support would in PLA.

Printers that only have one extruder head print support in the same material as the rest of the model. Printers that have multiple extruders can lay down support in another color to make it easier to see small areas of support and then pick them off (although one could argue that this is a bad idea because any support you fail to pick off will be more visible). Even better, a dual extruder printer can use one of its extruders to lay down a dissolvable filament. Chapter 7 discusses the options for this type of filament and the processes used to dissolve various types.

▒ **Tip**   Try to avoid support in tight spaces where it is difficult to pick out, or deep inside a model. If possible, put the support on a smooth surface where it will peel off. Try to have the support attached in the least-visible possible place.

Avoiding Support by Cutting a Model into Pieces

For an object with a complex surface that requires support, sometimes you can cut the object into two or more pieces, print the pieces cut-side-down, and then glue the parts together later. Some CAD programs have tools to make this sort of cut. If the program you are using does not, there are a few free or open source programs that allow the user to rotate an object around all three axes and then make a cut along a resulting convenient axis. Because this is a rapidly evolving area, search online for "cutting STL files free software." Often printed support can be avoided entirely with one judicious cut.

This technique is often useful too if the 3D-printed model is being used to make a mold. This technique does have its own issues, though. For example, if your platform is not very flat, or if the first layer warps up a bit, the two halves may have a gap. Figure 5-7 and 5-8 show the same model as in 5-5, but printed in two pieces and then put together. Glue and a bit of post-processing could make the joint in Figure 5-8 a lot less visible; this figure just has the two pieces balanced on top of each other on a pillow.

Figure 5-7. *The two halves of the creature also shown in Figures 5-2 and 5-5*

Figure 5-8. *The two halves from Figure 5-7 balanced onto each other (note the seam)*

■ **Tip** If you want to slice your model in two (or more) pieces to avoid support, use Meshlab, Meshmixer, or another program (see Chapter 4) to slice it up. Then delete the original STL file by selecting it and using your computer's Delete key, and import the two pieces.

Bridging

It is possible to bridge across open areas in a model without support if the open area is not too wide (say, under 20 to 30 mm). There are several schools of thought about the best settings to use when bridging across a gap. On the one hand, having the printer move more slowly than usual while trying to increase filament flow rate slightly may result in the bridge sagging a little. Conversely, having the printer move faster and pushing out less may mean the filament will not stretch enough to cross the open area and will break. Ideally, the filament should be stretched taut to avoid sagging, but not quite enough to break. Finding an optimum between the two requires some experimentation with your particular printer and filament combination.

Slicing programs will usually allow setting a speed specifically for bridging. For example, on Deezmaker printers, it is recommended that bridges be laid down at about 15 mm/s. Slic3r also has a setting to adjust the flow of plastic (relative to the rate of x/y motion) to control how much the plastic is stretched while leaving the nozzle. Defaulting this setting to the rate the slicing program creates based on optimum volume is a good place to start.

Another way to get around bridging is to terrace or arc under the bridged area so that the printer is in fact just climbing a 45-degree (or shallower) slope underneath. An overhang climbing at about a 45-degree angle is about the limit that can be printed without support. However, sometimes a steeper slope will work; a bit of experimentation is often worthwhile to avoid the need for support, particularly in a complex structure. In some cases, you may just get a few loops of "drooled" filament that you can easily cut off.

Tolerances

3D printers print all of one layer in one plane parallel to the build platform and then step up and do the next layer. In some cases, the extruder head moves upward, away from the platform after completing each layer. In others, the extruder may be fixed, and the build platform drops down a step at a time. Usually the two axes in the plane of the platform are referred to as x and y, and the vertical axis is the z-axis. *Layer height* is defined as the thickness of the material in each step up of the z-axis.

An extruder nozzle has a fixed diameter (like a garden hose), but by adjusting the rate of extrusion, you can press the extruded plastic between the tip of the nozzle and the platform (or the previous layer) to make it slightly wider. An extruder never lays down a line of filament with a perfectly round cross-section—otherwise, it would not have enough contact to adhere to the previous layer. The top of the layer also flattens when the end of the nozzle (as it lays down the next layer) presses down on it. Thus each layer put down will have a squashed or flattened oval (flat on top and bottom) cross-section, narrowest in the z direction. The slicing programs take into account the requested layer height and extrusion width and figure this out without user intervention.

As the layer height diminishes, the flattened part becomes larger relative to the curved outer part of the layer. Figure 5-9 illustrates this somewhat counterintuitive result. These squashed layers make the surface appear smoother in the z direction than it would be with stacked round cross-section layers. In other words, the radius of curvature of the rounded "ends" of the layer becomes smaller as the layers get thinner. As the layers trend toward (unachievable!) infinitely thin layers, the outer surface approaches the ideal intended perfectly smooth surface. In practice, though, the ideal surface line runs through the rounded ends of the squashed layer. The faint gray box around the layers in Figure 5-9 is this ideal surface.

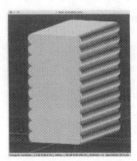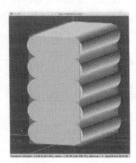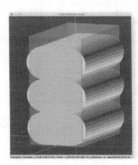

Figure 5-9. *Effect of layer height on single fused filament cross-section layer heights of 0.1 mm, 0.2 mm, 0.3 mm, and 0.4mm, all with a 0.5mm extrusion width. The faint grey box is 1 mm tall*

▓ **Tip** If you know the basic step size of your printer's z axis, which is dependent on both the stepper motor and the pitch of the leadscrew (or less frequently, timing belt), using a layer size that is an even multiple of that step size will give the best results. Typical motors have 200 steps/revolution, and M8x1.25mm-pitch (6.25-micron full-step) and M5x.8mm-pitch (4-micron full-step) are common leadscrews used in RepRap-style machines. If you have a 4-micron (0.004 mm) step size, a 0.1 mm layer height should work very smoothly, but a 0.15 layer height may not.

Thinner layers in the vertical (z) direction do not particularly affect the width of the line being put down in the x and y (build platform plane) dimensions, because printers manage how much filament they are pushing through the nozzle. In the real world, imperfections creep in that can cause issues and rougher vertical surfaces than would theoretically be possible. Although some of them are inherent in the design tradeoffs made by manufacturers of a particular machine (and thus are beyond the ability of a user to fix), taking some preventative steps can pay off in a better print. Although print quality increases with thinner layers, prints with thinner layers take longer to print because when the layers are thinner, you have to print more of them.

▓ **Caution** Layer height has to be less than (not equal to!) the nozzle diameter.

▓ **Tip**   If you are creating a print that has pieces that will fit into each other, you may have one of two situations. If you are trying to be sure that something will pass freely through something else, the tolerances may not be all that critical, and making the tolerances a little looser is probably a good bet. If, however, you want to have parts that mesh with each other without sticking, you will need to figure out the true tolerances you can practically achieve. A little trial and error may be needed, but one layer height all around is a good starting point (double the layer height for the margin on a hole diameter).

Speed

Printing speeds are typically measured in units of millimeters per second (mm/s). This is the rate of horizontal movement along the x/y plane, known as the *feedrate*. The slicer specifies the amount of plastic (traditionally in millimeters of filament pushed into the extruder, but some machines are now moving to volumetric extrusion, in which the slicer specifies cubic millimeters of material) to be extruded for each segment of motion, and the firmware calculates the appropriate speed to turn the extruder motor. Slicing programs typically allow users to set various different standard speeds (for printing perimeters, support, and infill, for example). Printer manufacturers typically suggest settings for these speeds, but different types of prints may work better with some adjustments.

Managing Internal Open Space

Just as there is open space around the outside of a model (like the statue's outstretched arm mentioned earlier), similar problems arise inside a model or in space enclosed by a model. Imagine a closed box: it would need some sort of support to run between the top and bottom. This support is called *infill*. Sometimes it is not necessary to have infill everywhere, and you can get away with just stringing filament across (usually) small gaps, a process called *bridging*. This section gives you some ideas about the design issues that arise with this internal support.

Perimeters

When an STL file is created, the triangles create a shell of the printable object. The space inside this shell is then partially filled in to make the object stronger and to create a base for the next layer as it is 3D printed. The outer surface defined by the STL file is called the *shell*. The material that the slicing software creates for this interior support is called *infill*.

Each layer of the shell is called a *perimeter*. The perimeter can be as little as one pass of the extruder thick or as many as specified. Two is typically a good number. The thickness of each perimeter varies, depending on the extrusion width set in the slicer (see discussion of this in the previous section).

Infill

Users of 3D printers do not usually want to create solid objects, because that uses a lot of filament. However, typically objects can't be hollow, either, because upper layers would be printed in air. As a result, most slicing software creates internal support called *infill* inside the solid surfaces of an object to minimize filament use (as well as to make the print faster). Figure 5-10 shows some of the common types of infill used by the MatterSlice engine, and Figure 5-11 shows some from Slic3r.

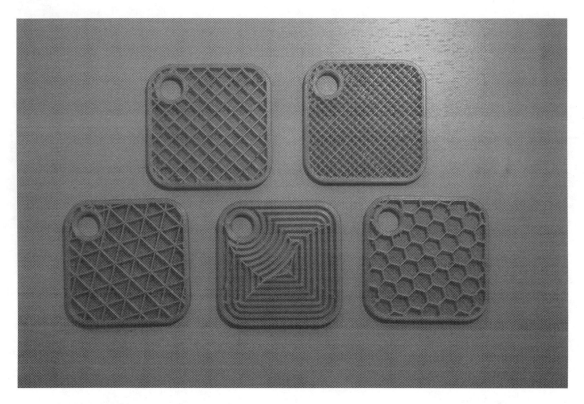

Figure 5-10. *Different types of infill available from MatterSlice: Top—Grid (R) and Lines (L). Bottom—Triangles (L), Concentric (middle), Hexagon (R)*

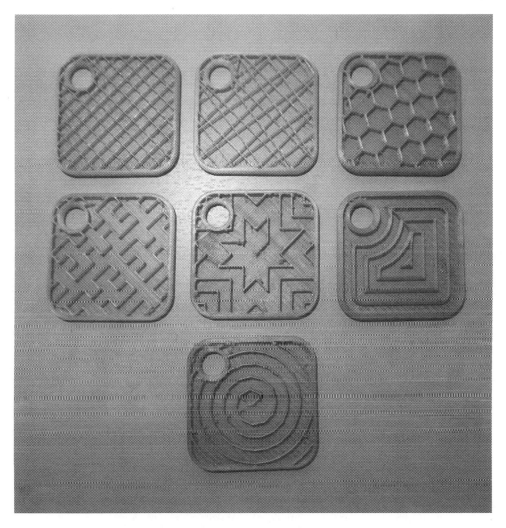

Figure 5-11. *Different types of infill available from MatterControl Slic3r: Top row, L–R—rectilinear, line, honeycomb. Middle row—hilbertcurve, octagramspiral, concentric. Bottom row—archimedean chords*

Another purpose of infill, and possibly the most important one, is to control shrinkage. Infill patterns are sparse enough to allow extrusions to stretch axially as they shrink radially so that they don't pull the perimeters inward as they cool and shrink. This can make 3D-printed parts maintain dimensional accuracy much better than injection-molded parts, which have to be designed with a significantly different size and shape from the final part in order to turn out the way the designer intends after shrinkage.

Print infill is usually specified in terms of percentage fill. The samples in Figure 5-10 were made with 25% infill, which means that 25% of the interior volume of the object is occupied by material, and 75% is open. (This percentage does not include the outer perimeter of the print.) The ones in Figure 5-11 use 10% with theoretically the same definition. However, clearly there is some difference in interpretation. Figure 5-12 shows a 10% MatterSlice grid versus the 25% one.

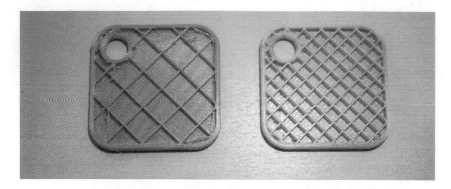

Figure 5-12. *10% and 25% MatterSlice infill patterns*

The choice of infill is determined by how strong the object has to be (and in what direction it needs to be strong). The size of the object can affect infill selection; if the object is really tiny, a high-percentage infill may be appropriate so that there is enough material to make the part sturdy. Objects with large, flat top surfaces may also need more infill so that the top solid layers can bridge over the empty space between infill lines.

Details, Details: Retraction

When a layer of a print has multiple separate islands of material—for example, when you are printing a standing person's legs—the extruder needs to be able to move between them without extruding. The problem with this is that extruding creates pressure in the nozzle, so that plastic keeps coming out after you stop pushing it. Thermal expansion and (to a lesser extent) gravity also tend to make the hot plastic inside the nozzle continue to slowly ooze out.

Printers solve this problem with *retraction*. When the printer finishes printing one island, before making a non-extruding move (called *travel*) to the next spot, it pulls the filament back a little to relieve the pressure in the nozzle. By retracting a little more, it is sometimes possible to create a bit of negative pressure to limit the oozing from thermal expansion and gravity, but it's important to move across the gap quickly. Therefore slicers will allow you to define a separate speed for these non-printing moves, which should generally be as fast as possible. On a machine with well-tuned acceleration and sufficiently strong motors, it may be best to just set this to a ridiculously high value and let the firmware limits cap the travel speed.

When there is not enough retraction, or the heated filament inside the extruder does not form enough of a seal to create negative pressure, you may get a thin strand of plastic stretched out across the gap that you are traveling across. This is called *stringing*. In the worst cases (no retraction at all), the strings may be almost as thick as the nozzle diameter, but it's more common to see extremely thin strings that are finer than a human hair.

Retraction is typically handled as an automatic feature in slicing software with some limited user control. For example, Slic3r has a check box to retract only when crossing a perimeter, and all of them have options to avoid crossing a perimeter (for instance, by going around a C-shaped island rather than just jumping straight across). This is a way to avoid retracting if printing sparse or complex infill might otherwise require it. It doesn't matter if infill strings a bit, because it will only be visible inside the model when the model is complete. Doing a lot of retraction can wear on the filament in some printer configurations and slows down the printing process, so avoiding it where possible is a big plus.

Learning More

As you have no doubt realized by now, we are scratching the surface here. As you get familiar with your printer and the types of prints you find yourself doing most often, you will no doubt begin to play with the other settings as well. Look at your manufacturer's documentation to be sure you stay inside the zones that are appropriate for your printer!

Summary

In this chapter you learned how to create "recipes" to slice your STL file and prepare it for printing. You saw some of the key settings that slicing software uses and what their implications are for 3D printing your project. The chapter walked through how to set up and use slice engines inside the MatterControl program.

This chapter covered the middle part of the overall 3D-printing workflow, bridging Chapter 4's development of a model on a computer screen and Chapter 6's hands-on interaction with the robotics of the 3D printer. Looking further forward, Chapter 7 covers filament-related settings in more detail.

CHAPTER 6

■ ■ ■

Controlling Your 3D Printer

In Chapters 4 and 5 we developed a model (an STL file) and sliced it to make it ready to print. We did not really talk much about what is in that sliced file (a .gcode file) and what to do with it. To carry forward the metaphor from Chapter 5, we will now turn on the oven and figure out how to actually "bake the cake."

At this point we start mechanically building parts versus creating idealized images of parts on a computer screen. This transition can lead to some surprises (and humbling experiences). The extruder and the build platform can get pretty hot, and things do not always turn out the way you would expect. Very often this will be an iterative process: you will start printing your file, discover that things are not going according to plan, and need to go back and reslice. It takes a little while to know your printer and develop some intuition—don't get discouraged!

■ **Tip** In this chapter you will read about many printer settings that can be tweaked during the process of making a 3D print work in the real world. Be methodical and change one thing at a time. Consider getting a little notebook (or making an online document) to write down what worked and what did not. Otherwise, it all blurs together after a while!

G-code and Firmware

Most open source, filament-using 3D printers are controlled with a series of commands, called *G-code*. Figure 6-1 shows how G-code flows through a typical open source printer. G-code loads onto the printer from a host computer via a USB port, although some printers have other options such as reading from an SD card. The *firmware* (software running on the printer itself) then interprets the G-code one command at a time and ships it off to the printer to execute. Status information (temperatures and the like) return to the user's computer through the USB. In some other cases a G-code interpreter runs on a host computer, and control signals are sent to the printer.

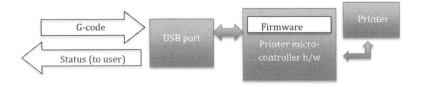

Figure 6-1. *Hardware and software architecture*

Many open source printers use Marlin firmware, which runs on Arduino-compatible microcontrollers. There is no operating system running on a microcontroller in system architectures like the Arduino. The processing hardware performs minimal command retrieval buffering and interpretation functions, and returns requested signals to the user. The shaded boxes in Figure 6-1 represent hardware; the unshaded boxes represent software and data. Although this architecture is the standard as of this writing, 32-bit ARM-based architectures may replace these less powerful ones.

Some printers can read G-code from an SD card rather than needing to use a USB port. The disadvantage there is that when running from an SD card the user's ability to monitor the printer in real time is limited. The MatterControl Touch tablet can also control a printer; more details about the tablet and cloud interactions are in Appendix B.

Understanding G-code

G-code is a very old programming language originally designed to control machine tools with a computer. Originating in the 1950s and 1960s, it has survived this long because of its flexibility and ability to run with minimal computing power. G-code is very low-level and is typically written such that all the commands are interpreted one at a time sequentially. Typical G-code functions include commanding an extruder to heat up to a particular temperature, instructing the printer to pause until an extruder reaches a certain temperature, moving the extruder to some (x, y, z) position, and conducting similar activities.

G-code for machine tools evolved gradually, with different dialects for each tool manufacturer. A standard of sorts called RS274D stabilized in the mid-1980s. Because the computer numerically controlled (CNC) market was pretty stable when the first low-cost 3D printers came along, a lot of the early users borrowed firmware and concepts to program those machines, and so a G-code dialect for 3D printers developed.

Each line of G-code commands the printer to do some small task or to set some parameter to a value that will be used for a task later on. For example, the snippet of code in the example that follows first sets the units that the firmware will use for calculation to millimeters (G21). It then tells the firmware to use absolute, not relative, coordinates (G90) and then commands the printer to move to position (3.000, 8.111, 4.444) while extruding filament such that 0.1234 mm of filament will have extruded when the command is completed (G1 X3.000 Y8.111 Z4.444 E0.1234). The firmware interpolates the movements required to get from one absolute position to the next and similarly determines how to feed the filament to extrude the requested amount before the next step. Millimeters of filament moved is currently the most common unit for the E values; but this may change to a volume measurement by the time you read this book.

```
G21
G90
G1 X3.000 Y8.111 Z4.444 E0.1234
```

M (Machine) Codes

Not all G-codes begin with G. For example, codes beginning with M are used (with some variation among manufacturers) for other mechanical functions, sometimes called *machine codes* (or some say, miscellaneous). M104 is commonly used in open source printers to set the extruder temperature to a particular value. M140 sets the temperature of heated build platforms—in this example, to 115 degrees C. M109 waits for the temperature of the extruder to reach the specified level, and M190 waits for the temperature of the heated platform to reach the specified temperature. An example of this sequence is shown in the following example. (Note that though the code is usually written as shown in the example, M109 and M190 do not need to have a temperature specified. If none is given, then the temperature that was set with M140 and M104 commands will be used.)

▓ **Tip**   Each line of G-code needs to be on one line (no newlines). A semicolon on the line makes the rest of the line a comment (see the example that follows).

```
M104 S210 ;comments here
M140 S115
M109 S210
M190 S115
```

Printers with multiple extruders need to address lines of G-code to the correct extruder. This is done with a *tool change* command, T. For example, in the case of most open source dual-extruder printers, T0 will select extruder 1, and T1 will select extruder 2 (following the common computing convention of beginning to count at zero). A T0 code will cause everything that follows to be executed on extruder 1. Some G-codes allow a Tx to be appended on the same line to show that just that command is for extruder x.

▓ **Tip**   A list of 3D-printer G-codes and a detailed discussion of their functions is available at http://reprap.org/wiki/G-code.

As you will see in the rest of this chapter, it is sometimes useful to be able to type in these low-level codes to debug possible hardware failures (such as blocked extruders, or a lack of connection to the printer) or to change the G-code built by your slicing program. Sometimes it is convenient to test that the printer is working correctly with a few simple commands rather than a complex G-code file. MatterControl has a *G-code Terminal*, a window that allows you to watch the codes being sent to your printer (and any responses) and also to send individual commands. We describe it in the next section.

Using MatterControl to Control Your Printer

As discussed in Chapter 5, MatterControl has the major advantage that it wraps around three slicing programs with somewhat different strengths (Slic3r, Cura, and MatterSlice) and allows you to select which one you use for slicing your file. In Chapter 5 we talked about how to slice a model, but not how to get that model onto your printer. Programs like MatterControl, which both allow you to slice a model and to actually control your printer, are called *host programs*. There are a few other open source hosts, notably Octoprint (http://octoprint.org), and various proprietary ones that are tied to particular closed-source printers.

Connecting to Your Printer and Starting a Print

Next, connect to your printer. If you previously set it up (Chapter 3), you should just be able to click CONNECT. Review the instructions in Chapter 3 under the MatterControl home screen for setting up a printer if you have trouble connecting. Your printer should show "Status CONNECTED" under it, as shown in Figure 6-2.

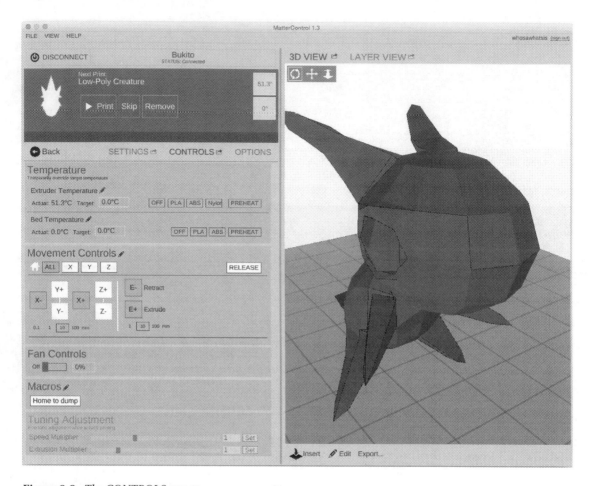

Figure 6-2. *The CONTROLS screen*

To run a print, first be sure that you have generated the G-code file and that you are happy with your settings (by clicking Generate in the LAYER VIEW) and looking carefully at the resulting file, as described in Chapter 5. Then just click on that item in the queue and click Print.

If, however, you need to do some other things (like change out filament, described later in the chapter), you may need the manual controls. Once you have connected, the controls to manually control your printer will be accessible. Click Settings & Controls (if you are in the screen that shows the print queue) and then CONTROLS. Figure 6-2 is a screen shot of the CONTROLS screen (and the accompanying LAYER VIEW), which we will now walk through. See the left side of Figure 6-2 to see how they look in the program:

- *Temperature*: This allows you to heat up (or cool down) your extruder and heated bed, if any. The display shows you both the target and actual temperature of both.

- *Movement Controls*: These controls allow you to move the printer in its three axes as well as push filament out of the extruder (E+) and retract it (E-). Note that if a printer is against an end stop, it will ignore a request to go beyond it.

- *Fan Controls*: If you want your printer's print fan (if you have one—*not* the fan that cools your extruder) to come on, you can turn it on here. Some printers have more than one fan, and one is intended to help manage cooling of the print, particularly for PLA prints.

- *Macros*: Your printer manufacturer may have supplied some macros—commonly used startup or shutdown tasks—that you can initiate.

- *Tuning Adjustment (Speed and Extrusion multipliers*: Sometimes you may want to increase the amount of plastic being put down (to make the print stick better, for example) or you may want to go faster or slower for a particular part of the print. These sliders allow you to do that.

▓ **Caution**   Be very careful when adjusting Speed or Extrusion multipliers. It is entirely possible to damage some printers by trying to drive too much filament through the extruder, or to move beyond design speeds. Be sure you know your printer's limits and make cautious changes.

When a Print Starts

When you have successfully sliced a part to create G-code and used a host program to send it to the printer, what happens next depends on what is in the G-code and also on the printer's firmware. If you are using a printer that has settings precoded into MatterControl, it is likely that there are several lines of G-code that are added to the beginning of every print to "home" one or more of the axes (to bring the nozzle to some known point on the platform), or these codes might be in the firmware. In either case, typically the printer will move the extruder to a predetermined starting point (usually off to one side) and will heat up the extruder and platform heater (if there is one).

After you tell the printer to run your G-code, you can watch the heaters kick in on temperature-monitoring box on the CONTROLS screen for the extruder or heated bed (if applicable). Once the extruder and platform reach the right temperature, the extruder will usually "drool" a little to get some filament melted before the print proper starts. Then the printer will start to print a skirt (if you specified one) and then your print. If you do not have a heated bed, the bed temperature should be set to 0 (do not try to get fancy and set it to room temperature, because you do not have a sensor to read anything and the printer will just sit waiting for its nonexistent thermistor to hit room temperature).

▓ **Tip**   MatterControl give estimates of build times in the LAYER VIEW window, which are generally indicative but may not be exactly right. This is because the firmware does not drive the extruder position at exactly the speeds specified in the G-code, but rather accelerates and decelerates each time it changes direction, making its average speed lower. These calculations occur in the firmware, so MatterControl may not have quite enough information to make a perfect prediction.

During a Print

Once a print starts successfully, there's not a lot to do except keep an eye on it in case something goes wrong. It's not a good idea to leave a 3D printer unattended, just as you would not go too far from a turned-on stove or oven. After a while, you will be able to tell from the sounds your printer makes if all is well. 3D prints can take a long time (many hours is common), and in the beginning you might try to do small tests of new techniques and materials so you can watch the proceedings actively and intervene if the print does not go as planned. Figure 6-3 shows what the CONTROLS screen looks like during a print.

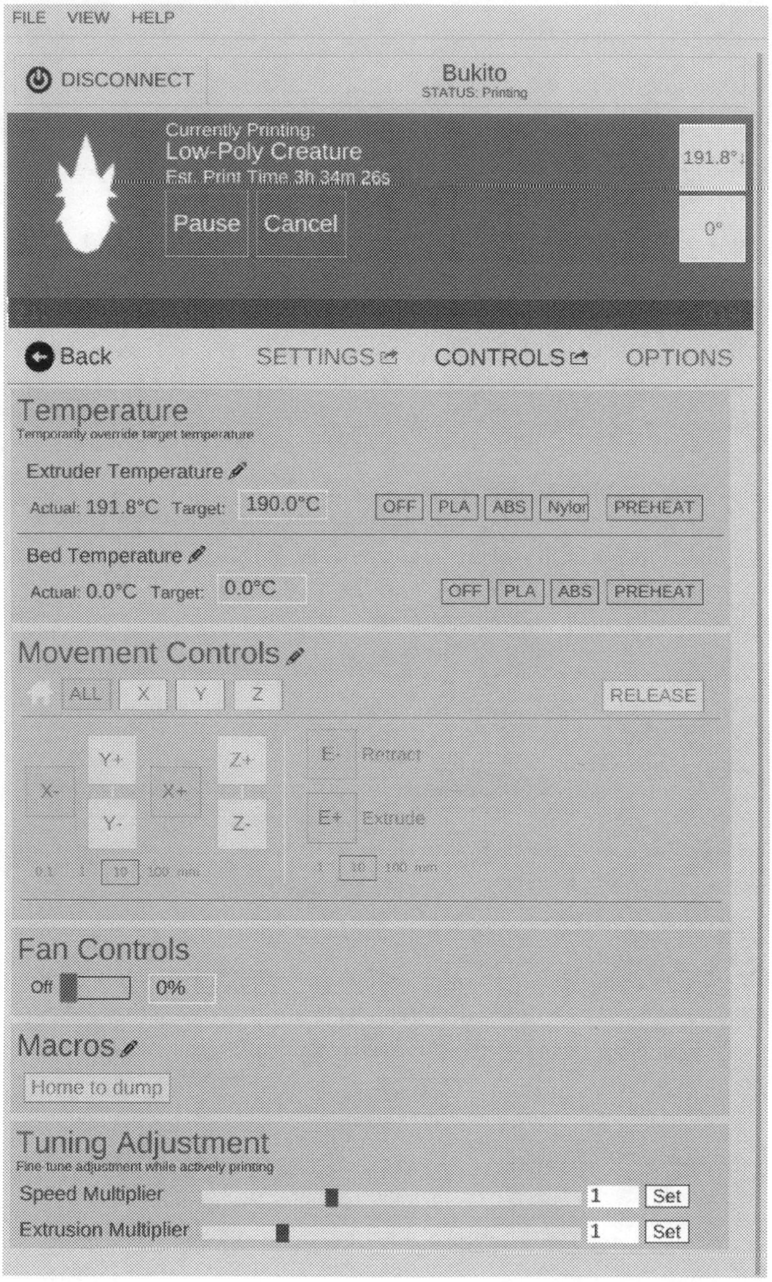

Figure 6-3. *The CONTROLS screen while a printer is running*

The most common failure is having the print come loose and slosh around. The only thing to do in that case is click CANCEL to kill the job and change some of the design to have a bigger footprint on the build platform—or perhaps print with a raft or brim, or modify the platform temperature. If a print just doesn't look right, go back to Chapter 5 and consider changing some of the slicing settings; look at Chapter 7 to see if the filament properties might be the problem; and consider Chapter 12's troubleshooting ideas if you suspect your printer. The platform may not have been adequately aligned and prepared.

▓ **Caution**   Do not disconnect your computer from the printer while it is printing if you are using MatterControl over a USB connection. You will stop the print, and there is no good way to restart.

When a Print Finishes Normally

When your part finishes printing, ideally the result will be a part sitting on the build platform looking just as you imagined it would. However, you still need to get the piece off the platform without breaking it. How do you get any support, brims, and so on off the part? And what should you do to be sure the printer is ready either to be turned off for the day or to print the next job?

▓ **Caution**   If your printer has a heated build platform, wait for it to cool down before you remove the part. Otherwise, the part (which is still a little soft) may bend or warp as you take it off.

Getting a Part off the Build Platform

Once the print has cooled down (see the preceding Caution), sometimes you can just grasp a part firmly and snap it off the platform. Usually, though, you need a little leverage to get it started. Keeping a part firmly attached is one of the more difficult issues in 3D printing, but sometimes the pieces adhere a little too well.

Unless your manufacturer recommends another implement, a common tool to pry pieces off the build platform is one of the tools used by artists: a paint knife, an artist's spatula, or a palette knife. These work well on blue and Kapton tape. Get one that is fairly stiff so that it is strong enough to move a substantial part. The exact form factor is a matter of taste and experience. Any art supply house should carry them (for example, Blick's, www.dickblick.com). While we are talking about small handy tools to have in your kit, you should also get a good pair of tweezers, which are useful for plucking bits of drooled filament out of places they should not be.

Picking Off Support and Cleaning Up The Print

If your part needed support, you now have to pick it off. This can be a painstaking process, and the precise procedure you use will depend on the tools you have available. Be careful because the plastic can be sharp; protect your eyes from the possibility of small flying sharp bits. Grasping the support with needle-nosed pliers and twisting it sometimes works well for sparse support; you will need to experiment and see what works for you. As discussed in Chapter 5, it's best to design your model in the first place to avoid big areas of support because they are very hard to remove.

Restarting or Shutting Off the Printer

When you take your print off the build platform, you can either turn off the printer or create your next print. If your manufacturer gave you slicing settings, it is likely that there are some shutdown lines of G-code in the standard setting, or the firmware may take care of some activities.

For example, a printer without a heated build platform may add a few lines to every G-code file like those in the following example. The first line turns off the extruder heater (sets the temperature to zero); the second line sends the *x* axis to its home (zero) position; and the last command disables all motors:

```
M104 S0
G28 X0
M84
```

In general, if a print finished normally, you probably can create or load in another G-code and just run the next job once you have cleared the platform. If you are not planning on using the printer again right away, it is best to turn it off and unplug it.

Managing and Debugging Problems

From time to time, you may suspect that your printer has a problem, or you may need to manually back out of an awkward failure that left the nozzle covered in stray plastic, or even stuck in the print. In those cases, you will want to use the Print or Control window in one of the host programs to send a G-code single line or two, or use the other manual controls that MatterControl provides. For example, what do you do if you want to change filament colors, but you forgot to pull out the previous filament when you turned off the printer (and now it is solidified in the nozzle)?

All the procedures that follow use the capabilities under Settings & Controls ➤ CONTROLS. MatterControl allows you to send a single line of G-code at a time, as well as move the extruder in any axis, heat the extruder, and heat the platform.

▓ **Tip** By default, most printers use degrees Celsius (C) for temperature and millimeters (mm) for length measurements. If you are having trouble thinking in millimeters, it might be helpful to know that there are about 25.4 mm in an inch, 210 degrees C equals 410 Fahrenheit, 115 C is 239 F, and 230 C is 446 F (to pick some commonly encountered temperatures).

G-code Terminal

During this type of circumstance you might want to see what G-codes are being sent to your printer, and perhaps send an individual code. You do this with the G-code Terminal, accessed through OPTIONS ➤ Hardware Settings ➤ Show Terminal. Figure 6-4 shows the result of these actions, in this case showing what is being sent to and echoed by the printer. You can also export some commands to look at later or to reuse.

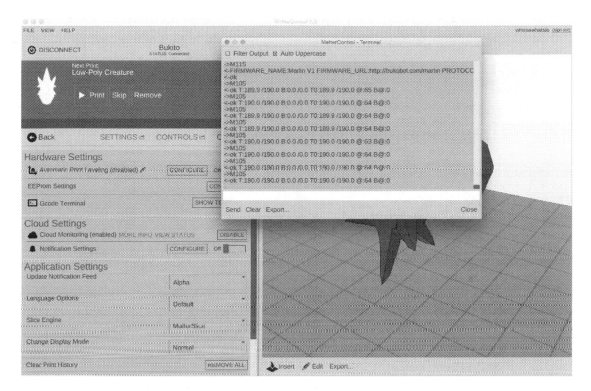

Figure 6-4. G-code terminal

Stopping a Print

Sometimes a print does not stick to the platform and starts to slosh around, or the print you thought would be fine without support isn't going to work after all, or you just look at what is building and scratch your head about how your lovely computer image could have turned out like that. When a problem like this becomes obvious, the best thing to do is click CANCEL. (MatterControl has a PAUSE option as well, but this is really intended for experts to be able to switch filament mid-print. If you try it, be aware that your nozzle is sitting there melting the print and may need a little priming to get going.)

If the print got jammed under the extruder somehow, you may want to move the extruder away manually (see the section "Backing Out of a Bad Situation") and then retract the filament. Once you get the failed print off the build platform, turn off the printer if you are not going to try again. Note that G-code to turn off heaters and other shutdown activities will not be executed if the job was killed partway through. Typically it's a good idea to cycle power on the printer just in case the partial print left it in some strange mode. If the failure rammed anything into the extruder, you might want to check that the build platform was not thrown out of alignment. Check your manufacturer's alignment instructions.

Changing Filament

When you finish printing a part, it's a good practice to retract the filament out of the nozzle so that you do not have to do get remaining filament out of the hot end, as we describe shortly. To retract the filament, as soon as the print job finishes, open the printer control panel and type in 10 mm of retraction. You can click the button to extrude 10 mm a few times; the filament should pop out of the input device after an appropriate number.

If you have a Bowden extruder (see Chapter 1), you only really need to get it out of the hot end to have the option of pulling it out easily later. Some printers also add commands to retract after every print job so you do not have to think about it. Even these printers, though, normally do not retract if you kill a job mid-print for some reason.

Suppose you forgot to retract the filament last time. You have bright pink ABS filament in the nozzle and you want to make an object in white in PLA. Do the following:

- Open the CONTROLS screen and in the Extruder Temperature box either type in the temperature appropriate to the *filament that is in the nozzle* (in this case, ABS, so about 230 degrees; see Chapter 7) or just click the ABS box.

- Look at the monitoring display and wait until the temperature is near the right level (but not all the way there, because then you will just melt more filament into the nozzle).

- Retract 10 mm at a time (click the E button with the box around the 10) until the filament springs out (or until you can pull it out the rest of the way, for printers that have a release).

- Then change the extruder temperature to the level appropriate *for the new filament* (in this case, PLA, so about 210 degrees). If there is plastic left in the nozzle, you need to purge it by pushing it out with the new filament. This has to be done at the higher of the two extrusion temperatures (in this case, 230 C). (If there is a big temperature difference between the two filaments, you might have to use an intermediate filament to purge out the old one, or use the "cold pull" technique described in Chapter 12 to clean it out.)

- Start the new filament into the extruder in whatever way is appropriate for your printer once the extruder is at the appropriate temperature (look at the temperature status graph).

- Once it is nearly in, extrude 40 mm or so.

- Keep extruding an additional 10 mm or so at a time until the filament stops coming out the old color. Using a skirt on your next print will take some of that away too, as discussed in Chapter 5.

- You can then run your next print with the new color and material.

▓ **Tip**　You could, in principle, use the preceding process to change out filament mid-run to have a multi-color or multi-material print with one extruder. Experts can and do try this (by using "pause"). It's very tricky, though, and results may be unpredictable.

Changing Temperatures During a Print

If a print looks like it may be having trouble sticking to a heated platform, you might want to raise the platform temperature just a few degrees. You can do this by going to the CONTROLS screen and changing the temperature. On the other hand, if the temperature is too high, the bottom layers may remain too soft, which will also allow it to peel up.

Basic Hardware Troubleshooting

Sometimes you'll want to determine whether a printer is having hardware issues of some type, so it's good to be able to try some basic commands to debug what is going on. This next section lays out some basic tests you can do to see what is wrong with your printer.

Checking Motion of One Axis at a Time

If you want to check the motion of one axis in a controlled fashion to see whether something is broken or loose, the movement controls section will allow you to move any axis in the positive or negative direction, in increments of 0.1, 1, 10, or 100 mm. In Chapter 2 you saw that the z axis is the vertical axis; x and y are in the plane of the build platform.

If nothing happens when you click on one of the movement directions, you may be at an end stop. Try clicking the button to move the same axis in the opposite direction. (For example, if nothing happens when you click $X-$, try clicking $X+$.) For the x and y axes, a 0.1 mm move may not be noticeable, but depending on the size of your printer and its current position, a 100 mm move might slam an axis into the limit of its travel. Some machines are also configured with software endstops, but the printer won't know its actual position if the motors have been disengaged. It is not uncommon for machines to refuse to move in the negative direction past the point where they were when the machine started up until it has been homed, because it thinks that that position is zero. You should always be able to home an axis, but be sure that the platform is clear before homing the z axis.

If you can't get any axis to run, you may have a connection problem; be sure your USB connector is firmly attached and that your printer hardware settings are correct for your printer.

Backing Out of a Bad Situation

If you forget to take a previous print off the platform, or otherwise do something you are not supposed to do, you may find the extruder jammed into a print or blocked somehow. Because it's hard to figure out which way is $+x$ and which way is $-y$ under battle conditions, you might want to familiarize yourself now with how your printer is set up in case you need to walk your way out of a problem with the manual controls.

Extruder Not Extruding

If the extruder is moving around but no material is coming out, there are a few possible problems. The extruder nozzle might be jammed, or the extruder motor might not be pushing out filament. To debug this problem, you may have to trick the printer a little to get the information you need.

Most printers are set up so that the drive system does not try to push filament through a cold extruder. However, for printers with a visible filament drive gear, it's helpful to see whether the gears are turning even though nothing is coming out. You may not be able to see anything if filament is stuck in the nozzle. But if no filament is in the extruder drive, you can send the following line of G-code to the printer to tell it to override the need to heat up the extruder:

M302

Then tell the gear to extrude a few tens of millimeters of filament. See if the gears are turning. If not, you have some other failure.

If the gears do turn, then your nozzle is probably clogged. To unclog a nozzle, follow your manufacturer's instructions. If your manufacturer did not provide any suggestions, you can try the following:

- Heat the extruder a little above what you used for your last print and try manually extruding, as we did for the filament-changing process earlier this chapter. If you have input an M302 command, be careful not to try to extrude any filament until the head is at the appropriate temperature.

- If nothing comes out, manually retract the filament. Take a look at the end of it—is there anything burned or strange on it?

- If not, try breaking off the end cleanly and extruding again.

- If all that fails, and your printer is able to accept nylon filament, try the "cold pull" procedure described in Chapter 12.

- You might also try searching online using the phrase "Unclog extruder *<your printer name here>*."

Running from an SD Card

A microSD card is a tiny removable storage device commonly used in digital cameras. Some printer firmware allows the printer to run G-code from a microSD or regular SD card. In either case, if you have a small screen on your printer, it probably will allow you to choose a file to run from an SD card.

For printers running Marlin firmware, if a G-code file named auto0.g is present on the SD card, the firmware will recognize it as a G-code you want to print and will automatically start running the code. This is convenient if you have a relatively mature G-code you want to run repeatedly (for demonstrations, for example) and you do not have a screen on the printer.

However, if you are running from an SD card, you may find yourself trotting back and forth to your computer a lot if you need to adjust the model or settings more than once. There is also no way to know how many layers are left to go, and no feedback about the temperature of the extruder and heated platform unless your printer displays that information on a small screen and/or allows you to have a USB cable plugged in while running from an SD card.

To kill a job running from an SD card, press your printer's reset button and then remove the SD card so that it will not auto-start again. Power off the printer if you are not going to try again, because G-code commands to turn off heaters and other shutdown activities will not be executed.

▓ **Caution**   If you have a printer that can use an SD card, be sure to remove it when you do use a USB connector to drive the printer from your computer. Otherwise, commands from a file on the SD card (such as auto0.g on a printer running Marlin firmware) may interleave randomly with whatever G-code you are sending from your computer, and nothing good will come of that.

MicroSD adapters that allow a computer to write on a microSD card from a USB port are available from places that sell office electronics or cameras. Do not remove the SD card while the printer is running; G-code is read and executed one line at a time. You will stop the print and have no way to recover.

Summary

In this chapter you learned how to load the model you generated in Chapter 4 and sliced in Chapter 5 onto the printer. This sliced model is known as a G-code file, and this chapter covers what is in a G-code file and how to manipulate one if needed. We focused on how to use MatterControl to control the printer manually both for actually printing and for debugging. In Chapter 7 you will learn about types of materials that we touched on in this chapter.

CHAPTER 7

■ ■ ■

Material Considerations

MatterControl is used by 3D printers that feed filament into an extruder, which melts the filament and lays it down a layer at a time. *Filament* is a thick thread made of a variety of thermoplastic materials and typically sold in one-kilogram spools, though some manufacturers sell other sizes. Figure 7-1 shows a one-pound nylon spool and a one-kilogram spool of polylactic acid (PLA) plastic.

Figure 7-1. *Typical spools of nylon (L) and PLA (R) filament*

This chapter covers the materials that a consumer filament-using printer can use, with a focus on non-proprietary filament. We discuss the types of materials available now, which applications are particularly suited for which materials, and things to think about when printing in one material versus another. We also show you how to configure MatterControl with settings for different materials.

An open source community effort is underway to develop a sticker for filament spools that would encode some of the printer settings. A system called the Uniform Filament Identification system (UFID) is under discussion in the user community to create a standard for these stickers. If this effort is successful (and if manufacturers accurately provide the information), a user may not need to be concerned about adjusting printer settings based on the material used because such information would be picked up by printers automatically. Until filament manufacturers implement such standards, though, users need to deduce and input various settings describing the filament diameter and the appropriate extruder and build platform temperatures.

Some filaments require a slower print speed than normal or special cooling settings to ensure that one layer cools before the next one is laid down. The settings suggestions in this chapter are typical; you may need to make adjustments based on experience with a particular filament/printer combination.

░ **Caution**   Build a small test object to try out settings for a new brand of filament before embarking on a many-hour big print.

Filament Quality Control

3D printers initially used filament that had been intended for welding plastic tanks. The filament diameter did not need to be very precise for that application, and so in the early days of filament-based 3D printers, the quality control on filament diameter was often inadequate. As the 3D-printer filament market grows, quality control is improving, but there are still occasional inconsistencies.

Common filament diameters are 3 mm and 1.75 mm. However, these are nominal diameters, and the actual diameter may vary. Many experts own a pair of calipers to measure the actual diameter for each manufacturer and check the filament diameter first if the printer seems to be laying down too much plastic or not extruding at all. If the diameter is bigger than the extruder is designed for, the printer may jam or stop extruding. To check the diameter of filament, use a pair of calipers. In fact, it is a good idea generally to have a pair of calipers available to check print results and compare prints to actual desired values.

If the filament diameter is too small, the print quality may be degraded. What is commonly sold as "3 mm" filament may actually measure around 2.87 mm or so. It is a bigger problem for filament to be too big than too small for printers that use 3 mm filament, so manufacturers aim for a nominal diameter in the 2.85 to 2.90 mm range, with 3 mm being an absolute maximum. 1.75 mm filament is typically in the 1.75–1.80 mm range. After you check the actual diameter of your filament, adjust the Settings&Controls ➤ SETTINGS ➤ Filament ➤ Filament ➤ Filament ➤ Diameter setting in MatterControl accordingly. You may want to save one filament preset per manufacturer. Sometimes different color filament from the same manufacturer or different batches from the same manufacturer can vary in diameter. The Diameter setting is available in the Standard and Advanced view, but not in the Basic one. Figure 7-2 shows the help explanation for this setting too (available if you check the Show Help box). See Chapter 5 for more on how to change a slice engine setting.

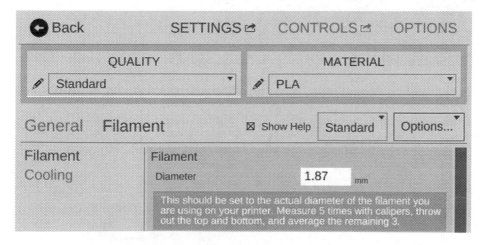

Figure 7-2.   *Filament diameter setting in MatterControl, Standard view*

Poor-quality filament may contain air bubbles, which result in erratic print quality. Worse, contaminant particles can block the extruder nozzle. If a printer suddenly starts having problems extruding, an erratic filament diameter or filament contaminants should be early suspects. Be sure to use 3D-printer filament, and not something that looks like it but was not intended for the purpose.

Can you start with raw plastic and make (or recycle) your own filament? Unfortunately, this is not as easy as it seems, largely because of the need for precision already noted. There is also always a risk that a raw plastic may have unexpected additives. There have been some entrepreneurial efforts to create desktop machines that make filament from raw material, but they are still at a pretty early stage. Track developments on crowdfunding sites like Kickstarter (www.kickstarter.com) if you want to pick up an experimental machine when they stabilize enough for your taste.

Filament-Related Settings in MatterControl

The last section touched on the filament diameter setting, but actually quite a few settings are under the Filament category. You have quite a few things to think about if you elect to use the Advanced level. We walk through them here one at a time, and then in the rest of the chapter talk about how to select values for some of the key settings. If you are in the SETTINGS area and select Filament ➤ Filament, you get the screen in Figure 7-3.

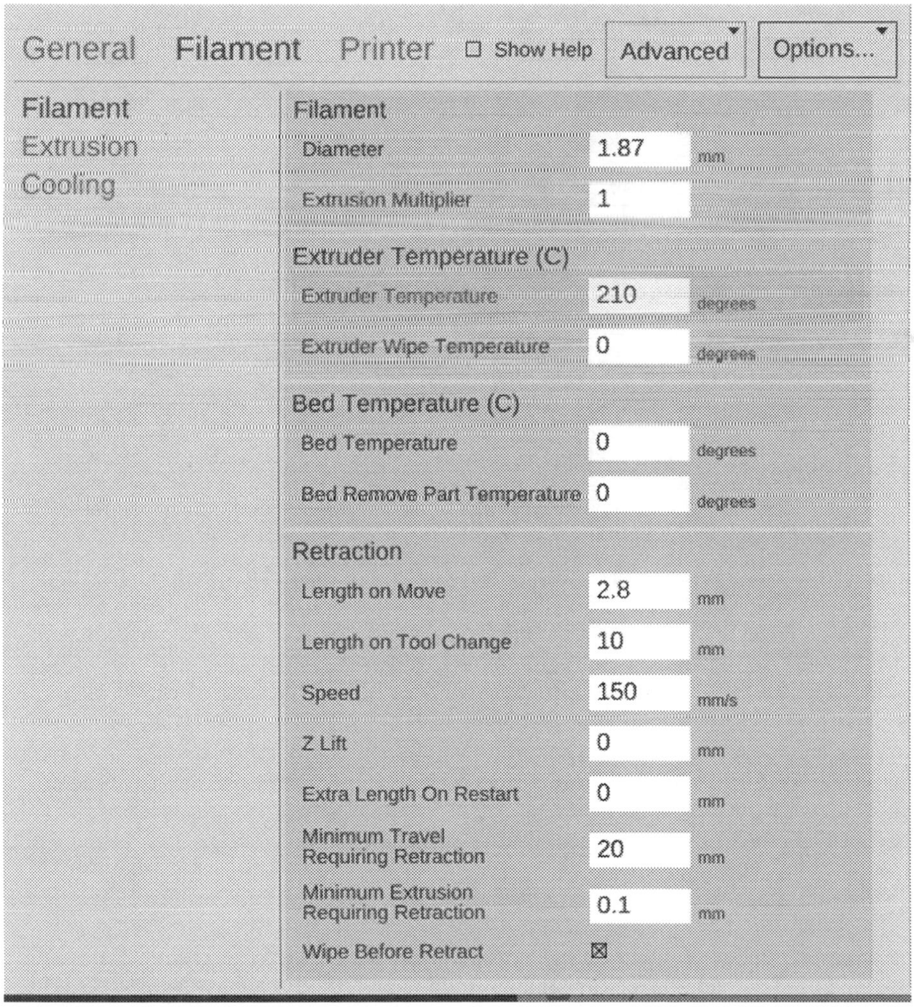

General	Filament	Printer	☐ Show Help	Advanced ▾	Options... ▾

Filament	**Filament**		
Extrusion	Diameter	1.87	mm
Cooling	Extrusion Multiplier	1	
	Extruder Temperature (C)		
	Extruder Temperature	210	degrees
	Extruder Wipe Temperature	0	degrees
	Bed Temperature (C)		
	Bed Temperature	0	degrees
	Bed Remove Part Temperature	0	degrees
	Retraction		
	Length on Move	2.8	mm
	Length on Tool Change	10	mm
	Speed	150	mm/s
	Z Lift	0	mm
	Extra Length On Restart	0	mm
	Minimum Travel Requiring Retraction	20	mm
	Minimum Extrusion Requiring Retraction	0.1	mm
	Wipe Before Retract	☒	

Figure 7-3. *Filament ➤ Filament Advanced settings in MatterControl*

The first section sets the filament diameter (discussed in the previous section) and the Extrusion Multiplier. Normally you would leave this at a value of 1—in other words, you would not change the default amount of plastic being extruded. Sometimes, for a particular effect, you may want to under- or over-extrude, but these circumstances are unusual. A more common use for this feature is to compensate for a printer with a slightly-off steps/mm setting for its extruder in firmware, or for variations in the depth to which the extruder's drive gear bites into the filament (which alters the effective diameter of the drive gear, and thus the effective steps/mm). Some printers require this type of adjustment more than others.

The next two sections set the Extruder Temperature and Extruder Wipe Temperature. The Extruder Temperature is the temperature that the extruder is set to for printing; values for common materials are shown in Table 7-1 later in this chapter, with an accompanying explanation for those materials. The Extruder Wipe Temperature setting is used by machines with a wipe procedure at the start of prints (for example, the Lulzbot Mini). Leave it at zero if in doubt.

Table 7-1. *Filament Characteristics*

Material	Print temperature (deg. C)	Bed temperature (deg. C)	Speed
PLA	210	60	Normal
		Unheated/blue tape	Normal
ABS	240	115	Normal
Nylon 618	240	Unheated/Garolite	Normal
HIPS	240	115	Normal
Elastomer	230–240	Unheated/blue tape, bare glass	Very slow
PET	Nominally 212–224; some users suggest 250	80	Slow
Polycarbonate	> 280	Very high	Varies

Similarly the Bed Temperature is the temperature to which you set your heated bed (if you have one). Leave it at zero if you do not have a heated bed. The Bed Remove Part Temperature only applies to printers that have a part-removal procedure at the end of their printing process. For the printer-specific settings, see what your manufacturer recommends.

The final grouping is made up of settings for retraction. *Retraction* is discussed in Chapter 5 (see the section "Details, Details: Retraction"), and generally speaking the best practice is to use your manufacturer's suggested values. If you have a print with thin vertical features, the movement of the traveling nozzle may break them while printing, but you can mitigate this by enabling Z-lift (which raises the nozzle slightly before performing fast travel moves). About half of your nozzle diameter is a good starting value for Z-lift. When Wipe Before Retract is enabled, filament is retracted and the hot end moves backward along the previously printed area for a few mm before moving to the next printing location. This allows the material that will ooze to be deposited in an area that is not noticeable, or is less noticeable, and can greatly reduce stringing. However, this tactic may increase the print time significantly if the print is made up of many tiny features that are separated by gaps that cause frequent retraction, and should be used judiciously.

Figure 7-4 shows the settings you can see when you are in Advanced mode and select Filament ➤ Extrusion. Increasing the First Layer Extrusion Width setting allows you to build the first layer out of wider extrusions that will adhere better to the print surface and will be less sensitive to a slightly uneven platform. Similarly, the support material can be tweaked with its setting to be made of thicker extrusions (if your support structures are breaking before they finish printing) or thinner ones (if they are too solid to break apart after printing). A value of zero tells MatterControl to use its default value based on other settings.

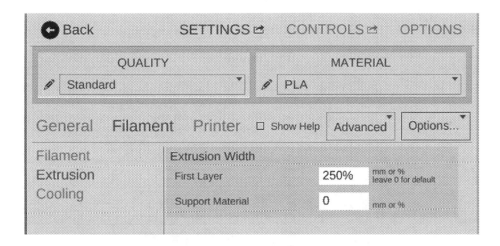

Figure 7-4. *Filament ➤ Extrusion Advanced settings in MatterControl*

Finally, Figure 7-5 shows the Advanced settings under Filament ➤ Cooling. The Fan Speed settings values refer to a fan aimed down at your print, if your printer has one. It does not refer to settings for any other fans you may have that cool an extruder or other parts of the printer. A little later in this chapter, the section "Ventilation, Drafts, and Cooling" (including Figure 7-6) talks more about these fans. It is probably best to use your printer default settings for these. The rest of the settings here control how your printer behaves with small layers that print quickly and thus do not have time to cool before printing the next layer. You have the option to slow the printing of a layer to give it more cooling time, along with a minimum speed setting to limit how much it can slow down. The Enable Extruder Lift feature stops printing, moves the nozzle away, and idles to allow time for cooling, but this is usually problematic because the plastic that is inside the nozzle during this time will tend to ooze out while it's idling.

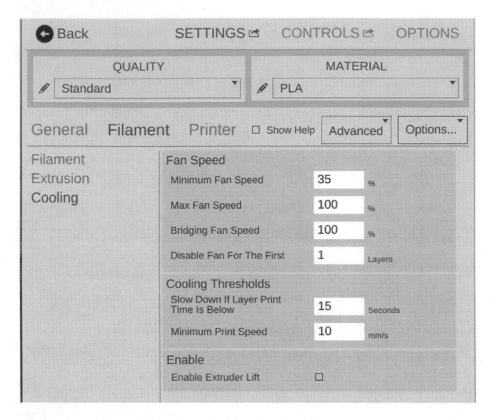

Figure 7-5. *Filament* ➤ *Cooling Advanced settings in MatterControl*

Selecting and Using a Filament

Selecting material for a project requires trading off many different factors based on the use of the object, available materials, and cost. Some 3D printers are only able to print in one material, and then the issue becomes whether it is possible to use that material for the intended purpose.

If your printer gives you some options, however, there are some significant differences in material properties among the common materials used by consumer-grade printers. Most 3D-printing materials are classed as *thermoplastics* (polymers that soften as they melt and then harden again when cooled) or *thermoplastic elastomers* (TPEs), which are a combination of a plastic and a rubber.

Common 3D-printing thermoplastics include polylactic acid (PLA), acrylonitrile butadiene styrene (ABS), and nylon. Depending on the characteristics of the extruder, printers may also be able to handle polyethylene terephthalate (PET) and polycarbonate.

There are also more exotic materials and mixtures for interesting esthetic effects. More types of filament are coming up all the time. This chapter does not presume to offer an exhaustive list, but rather is an attempt to sample some typical and up-and-coming options.

Looking at the manufacturer's specifications for any given filament is a good idea. Numbers given in this chapter are typical numbers. Some extruder hot ends, however, may have an upper temperature limit below that needed for some of the materials mentioned here.

■ **Caution** MatterControl does not check to see whether a user is exceeding the upper limits of any given printer model. Printer firmware may or may not catch attempts to exceed limits. Be sure to check the manufacturer's specifications before setting up for any particular extruder and bed temperature.

The following sections lay out some of the key considerations when choosing a material to make your object and when printing in that material. First you need to think about whether the material is strong enough at all, and how to orient the print to take advantage of the fact that a 3D-printed part will be stronger along a layer than across layer boundaries. We talk about issues that arise when printing in different materials—whether a heated bed is required, whether drafts are a problem, and whether you might need to print more slowly with some materials.

Directional Strength

How strong is something made on a 3D printer? The answer depends on the filament material, but also on the details of the print. Prints are weakest in the z direction (because the layers can pull apart), so the orientation of a print on the print bed also has implications for strength of the printed object. Design of an object should take into account the following:

- The inherent strength of the material
- Whether the object's operating environment will get hot
- Whether the object's operating environment will contain any chemicals that affect the material
- The direction in which the object will need to be strongest
- Support structure needed in various build orientations
- Thickness of the outer shell of the model
- Infill pattern and density
- Any connections with other (non-3D-printed) parts
- Brittleness—the ease with which a part (particularly a small part, or support) will break off
- Tolerances and clearances

As discussed in Chapter 5, many settings in slicing software specify the external and internal structure of a part. Chapter 10 discusses some typical case studies to make how these factors interact more concrete.

The Right Print Bed

Prints need to stick solidly to the build platform so that they do not shift or fall off while the piece is printing. On the other hand, the platform or the print may be damaged if the print is stuck down too firmly.

For many materials (including ABS and polycarbonate), the platform has to be kept warm so that the print sticks to it. Some 3D printers have heated platforms; ones that do not probably cannot print in these materials. Materials that need a heated bed will warp while printing if the bed is not adequately heated. As the lower layers cool, they shrink and pull up from the bed at the corners. The hot layers on top are a bit bigger, and as they cool the part warps more and more as the upper layers also contract.

Beyond heating, the surface of the platform needs to be a material that is compatible with the print material. At the moment, figuring out what sticks to what is fairly empirical. Blue painter's tape (3M seems to work best) and high-temperature Kapton tape (transparent gold-colored tape) are common printer bed materials. Glass, often with glue or some other adhesive coating, is becoming a more popular printing surface. Follow your manufacturer's directions, but generally the following rules of thumb hold:

- PLA will stick well to blue painter's tape. Typically, we think of this tape as something that pulls off a wall easily, but interestingly, the 3M tape in particular seems to be just the right surface for PLA to stick to sturdily. Blue tape is available in wide rolls that can cover a smaller print bed in one shot, which avoids tape edge lines in the first layer of the print.

- PLA does not need a heated bed if the print bed is covered with blue tape. However, if the bed is covered with something else (for example, Kapton tape), the bed may need to be heated to a relatively low temperature to make the model stick.

- If you have a heated bed covered with Kapton tape and you decide to try blue tape on top to print PLA with the bed cold, be sure the bed is cold and put on the blue tape at right angles to the Kapton so that it does not tear off the Kapton when you remove it. Blue tape also tends not to stick to Kapton tape as well as it does to bare glass, and the PLA parts warp enough to pull up the tape.

- Nylon does not like to stick to many materials. Garolite LE (a material made from phenolic resin with embedded linen fibers) is a good material for print beds used for nylon. Some printer manufacturers sell a Garolite platform that can be switched out instead of (or on top of) a heated platform.

- Other materials (such as ABS) do well on a heated bed covered in high-temperature tape (such as Kapton tape). Some printers come with glue sticks or other materials to enhance printed part adhesion. Experiment a bit to see what works for your printer and the parts you are printing.

Ventilation, Drafts, and Cooling

There are few standard formulations for materials for 3D printing just yet, so it's generally a good idea to ventilate the area around your 3D printer. Some materials (such as ABS) smell fairly strongly, so think about who and what else is nearby when using the printer.

However, direct airflow on a printer when it is printing can be either a positive or negative thing (PLA often does better when cooled with a small fan, but ABS needs to be kept warm). It is usually best to ventilate by pulling air away from a printer rather than blowing air onto it. Generally airflow onto a print should be carefully directed and controlled with a fan, and you should avoid printing in the presence of erratic or unpredictable drafts.

Figure 7-6 shows a PLA fan on a printer cooling a print. The PLA fan is the small round object held on with two cable ties.

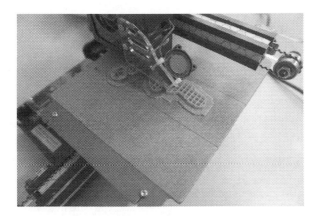

Figure 7-6. *A PLA fan cooling an object*

Storing and Handling Filament

Most filament is *hygroscopic* (it absorbs water from the air) to various degrees, which can affect its properties and the quality of a print. Keep spools of filament dry and avoid extreme temperatures. If you buy a spool of filament and are not going to use it for a while, keep it in the original sealed package until you are ready to use it under environmentally stable conditions. It is probably unwise to store it in a damp garage that gets very hot in summer, for example. If you can keep it sealed up in a cool place with some dessicant packages, that is best. Nylon in particular has issues with humidity, and ABS does too, although not as severely.

▓ **Tip** Before you begin a print, be sure filament loops do not cross over or under each other on the roll. Try to loosen the filament a little so it is not overly tight, particularly if you are starting a print near the end of a roll. If the filament knots in place even briefly, it can pull on the extruder and affect print quality (or stop the print). A plastic lazy susan (from a kitchen supply store) works well if it is the right diameter to carry the filament roll. Back in Chapter 1, Figure 1-1a shows one of these off to the side of the printer. If you want to make your own, there are many different filament-carrying devices on the STL download sites mentioned in Chapter 4.

Temperature and Speed Settings

When you print in a particular material, there are three major settings to worry about: temperature of the extruder (known as *print temperature*), temperature of the heated bed (or absence of a heated bed), and the speed of printing. Table 7-1 lists some typical values for materials that are discussed later in this chapter. Chapter 5 covers printer settings in more detail along with the effects of the geometry of the object being printed, but Table 7-1 will give you a sense of the relative difficulty of printing with some of these materials. These are only examples, though, and different formulations and printers may perform best with significantly different settings.

Will My Filament Spool Run Out During My Print?

Filament is fairly expensive, so you want to use every bit on the spool if you can. However, you also do not want to run out during a print. MatterControl gives an estimate of the length of filament that will be used in the print. When you get near the end of a roll, pull some out, measure it, and note roughly what fraction of the remaining filament remains after subtracting that part. That will let you estimate whether your print will work or not. For example, if you pull out a meter and it's about a quarter of what is left on the spool, you have four meters of filament left. If your print says it will take 3,900 mm (3.9 meters), you should start your print with a roll with more filament on it.

Filament Materials

The following sections describe a few of the common materials in a bit more depth. PLA, ABS, and nylon are currently the most frequently encountered filaments, but we talk about a few of the more exotic ones, too.

Polylactic Acid (PLA)

PLA is one of the more common materials for 3D printing. It is typically made from corn or similar renewable materials and is biodegradable. It can be extruded at a relatively low temperature (around 210 C), which means it is less challenging to make an extruder print PLA than other materials. Printing PLA does not require a heated bed. The downside is that it becomes soft at hot-car-dashboard temperatures, so a little thought needs to go into when it is and is not a good idea to print something in PLA.

That said, PLA is a very versatile material that is generally fairly forgiving to print. Many printers have a small fan to cool PLA as it prints to improve print quality. It can be difficult to get support off cleanly with PLA prints (see the discussion in Chapter 5) because the material is still fairly ductile when cold and so does not snap off cleanly. Slicing algorithms in this regard are steadily improving, though.

PLA comes in many colors and opacities, and even in a version that changes color from white to bright purple when exposed to UV light (like sunlight).

▧ **Tip**   People have also been experimenting with using PLA in the ancient *lost wax* technique for making metal and glass objects. This is discussed in Joan's previous book, *Mastering 3D Printing* (Apress, 2014).

▧ **Caution**   Because PLA becomes soft at a relatively low temperature, it is unwise to use PLA for any application where the printed part might get warm. For example, it's not a great idea to print critical parts of a RepRap printer (Chapter 1) in PLA and then put the printer in an un-air-conditioned room during a heat wave.

Filled Materials

There are a steadily increasing number of proprietary material blends that will print with settings like those for PLA. These are thermoplastics infused with other materials to give interesting printed material properties.

LAYWOO-D3 is a thermoplastic infused with finely ground wood. Varying the temperature a little during printing will give the print a wood-grained appearance. Thin-walled prints in LAYWOO-D3 can be a little fragile. Similarly, LAYBRICK is a thermoplastic infused with milled chalk to look like stone when printed.

Filaments made of PLA infused with bronze, copper, stainless steel, magnetic iron, and carbon fiber all exist, although they can be challenging to print with. These filler materials can make a print look like wood or metal, and metal-filled filaments are also significantly denser, making them feel more like metal. However, they do not give prints the other properties of those materials. Metal-filled plastic will not be significantly stronger or more tolerant of heat than plain plastic, and the filler material may even weaken the plastic-to-plastic bonds slightly.

Carbon fiber filament is produced by chopping the fibers up into tiny pieces that will go through the nozzle without clogging, but without long, contiuous fibers, it cannot add much strength to the PLA base material. These fibers also do not cross layers, so they cannot affect strength in the weakest direction. Thus prints with carbon fiber filament are reported to be a bit stiffer but more brittle than prints with infilled PLA. If strength, abrasion resistance, or other mechanical properties are important for your part, be sure to test appropriately. These filaments can abrade your nozzle fairly quickly and be prone to clogging the nozzle.

It is now becoming possible to print conductive elements using conductive filament, such as that available from Proto-Pasta (`www.proto-pasta.com`). Like other filled materials, this is a carrier of PLA infused with somewhat conductive materials, such as carbon black. These conductive filaments can be embedded in other printed objects (by using a printer with two or more heads, as described in Chapter 8) or attached to other surfaces to make circuit elements. This process generally does not produce materials that are conductive enough to carry any significant electrical current, but they may be useful for capacitive sensors or for protecting components from static electricity. There are now also more experimental machines being built to print with silver inks that may make 3D-printed circuits more viable in the near future.

Finally, there are some filaments that are infused with glow-in-the-dark materials, and new filled materials are an active area of development for filament manufacturers. The possibilities there are pretty endless.

Acrylonitrile Butadiene Styrene (ABS)

ABS is another common consumer printer filament material. You may know it best as the plastic used to make many toys (including LEGO bricks). It is a hard and durable plastic and stays strong at higher temperatures than PLA does. However, it does tend to warp when cooling and is challenging to print without a heated bed. ABS is also a good choice for parts that need a lot of support because support typically will snap off more cleanly in ABS than in other common materials.

Nylon

Nylon is a versatile material because thin nylon structures are flexible but thicker ones are fairly stiff and strong. Nylon is often a good choice for functional parts, but you need to be careful to think through the directions of the layers and where the part is weakest. Nylon 618, 645, and 680 are a few of the formulations available from the manufacturer Taulman (the numbers refer to the molecular structure of the particular formulation).

With nylon, it is particularly important to be certain that you are getting 3D-printer filament. Other products out there (such as weed-whacker filament) may appear similar but may contain nozzle-clogging impurities or materials that give off toxic volatiles when heated. Nylon filament is particularly prone to absorbing moisture from the air. Keep nylon filament dry. When you start to print nylon, small puffs of steam come from the extruder that can be startling if you do not expect it.

Nylon typically comes in white filament, but pieces printed in nylon can be dyed with dye appropriate for nylon fabrics. Nylon requires a high-temperature nozzle and a special unheated platform surface (for example, Garolite) and so may be beyond the capability of your printer.

▓ **Caution**   Be sure the filament you buy is intended for use in 3D printers. Do not go on appearances alone. The chemistry and material composition of the filament is important both for print quality and your safety during printing (review the safety and ventilation section in Chapter 2).

Polyethylene Terephthalate (PET)

PET or PETG (the G stands for Glycol-modified) is a clear plastic commonly used in water bottles. It is sold in 3D-printer form by several manufacturers. PET is a plastic that is approved by the U.S. Food and Drug Administration for direct contact with food. As of this writing, Taulman (the makers of t-glase, www.taulman3d.com) has said on its website that the company is awaiting direction on the rules for declaring a part printed with t-glase to be food-safe.

PET is transparent. A 3D-printed part will not be perfectly clear in all directions because of the layer lines, but will be translucent, particularly in thin-walled objects. It has a relatively low melting point and thus should not be used for parts that will be in hot environments.

Polycarbonate

Polycarbonate is a very strong material but is still somewhat experimental for consumer 3D-printing use. Polycarbonate can be challenging to print because it is difficult to get to stick to the build platform. But if you are at the more industrial end of the printing spectrum, polycarbonate is a developmental material to watch for the future. Be sure to read the filament manufacturer's documentation and consider your printer's limitations carefully.

Thermoplastic Elastomers (TPEs)

Elastomers are combinations of a thermoplastic and a rubber. Prints made with a TPE (such as NinjaFlex) are strong and flexible. However, the print has to be created very slowly to avoid buckling the filament during printing. This is more challenging with 1.75 mm filament than 3 mm because the thinner filament tends to flex and be difficult to manage. Bowden extruders can exacerbate this problem because the filament may flex too much between the drive gear and the nozzle.

Once these challenges are overcome, however, the unique qualities of TPEs will probably enable a lot of new applications of 3D printing. Thin TPE prints can be crumpled in your hand like a thin rubber mat, and thicker-walled prints are like shoe soles—tough yet flexible.

Dissolvable Support Materials

As discussed in Chapter 5, removing support material can be difficult, and we try to avoid it where we can. However, if it cannot be avoided and the part requires a lot of support that would be awkward to remove, dissolvable support is a good option. As the name implies, you print the support material with something that will dissolve when you are done. To use it, you need to have a printer with more than one extruder—one for the primary material and one for the support. Chapter 8 talks more about these. High-impact polystyrene (HIPS) is a common dissolvable support material. It dissolves in d-Limonene, a common solvent.

Of course, a water-soluble support material would be ideal. PVA, or Polyvinyl Acetate, is sometimes marketed as a water-soluble support material. Because it is water-soluble, protecting it from atmospheric moisture is particularly important. PVA may harden permanently if left in a hot extruder, and in our experience it tends not to stick adequately to anything, including itself. For these reasons, we recommend against trying to use it as a support material for now, though work is being done to develop formulas that are more appropriate for 3D printing.

Summary

In this chapter you learned about the different types of filament, their material properties, and the settings that MatterControl needs you to define so that the program can slice your model correctly. We also discussed the best filaments to use in particular design situations. Chapters 8 reviews some special situations such as printers with two or more extruders, and Chapter 10 goes some case studies, so that you can see in context how to think about the best choice of material for a given job.

CHAPTER 8

■ ■ ■

Special Cases

The last three chapters talked you through the process of creating a 3D model, running slicing software to create printer commands, and finally loading it onto a printer and running it. This chapter goes into a few situations that are a little different than the straightforward one of creating a solid object. What happens if you want an object that is hollow inside (no infill), or that is shaped like a vase (solid bottom, but no infill or top)? And how do the directions we have given so far extend to 3D printers that have more than one extruder, to print in multiple materials? We go through an example of each in this chapter.

■ **Note**   Be sure you have the Advanced view on in the Settings & Controls ➤ SETTINGS panel for the activities in this chapter.

Printing Hollow Objects

As a 3D print builds up a layer at a time from the bottom, upper layers need to be supported by ones below them, just like a brick wall. Material that is supporting something outside the surface of your object (and that you will want to removed later) is discussed in the section "Supporting and Orienting a Model" in Chapter 5. We talked about material that supports and strengthens prints internally in the "Infill" section in Chapter 5. What happens if you would like to design something that is hollow, either for an aesthetic reason (say, if you were printing with translucent filament and you did not want the infill to show through) or to save filament?

The actual process of making something hollow is straightforward from the software's point of view. Go to Settings and Controls ➤ SETTINGS ➤ General ➤ Infill and set Fill Density to 0. You will need to think about whether you want to make the walls of your object a bit thicker, though, to make up for the absence of infill. You can do that by going to Settings and Controls ➤ SETTINGS ➤ General ➤ Layers/Surface ➤ Outer Surface-Perimeters and increasing the perimeter count to 2 or 3, unless you want the print to be delicate and translucent. You can print with a single perimeter, but it can be tricky. To be sure your print sticks and is sturdy, you may want to go to Settings and Controls ➤ SETTINGS ➤ General ➤ Layers/Surface ➤ Outer Surface – Top & Bottom and set Top Solid Layers and/or Bottom Solid Layers to a bigger number than you usually use. (In general, we tend to use two perimeter layers, and at least four bottom and six top solid layers for most prints.)

As we saw in Chapter 5's "Bridging" section, a carefully designed 3D print can in fact angle outward with layers offset a bit from each other (up to about a 45-degree angle in the resulting surface) or have small completely unsupported parts. A hollow object is obviously going to be more fragile than one that is supported. To anticipate problems in a hollow object, you should spend some time in MatterControl's Layer View walking through how it will print. You can do this by using the 2D View and moving up a layer in a time to see if (simulated) islands of printed matter are suddenly appearing in upper layers that had nothing below, or if you prefer, the 3D View, although it can be harder to see sudden appearances of material there. You can also (externally) support hollow print, but be very careful taking the support off!

Figures 8-1 and 8-2 show the MatterControl 3D Views of a hollow 1940s-style toy rocketship designed by Rich, halfway up and finished. Figures 8-3 and 8-4 show it printing and completed. It was printed with no support, but with a brim to hold it on the platform. The angles were designed so that the 45-degree rule was never exceeded. In the pictures of the print you can see that there was a little bit of ooze while traveling between the leg structures, but nothing that could not be clipped off later.

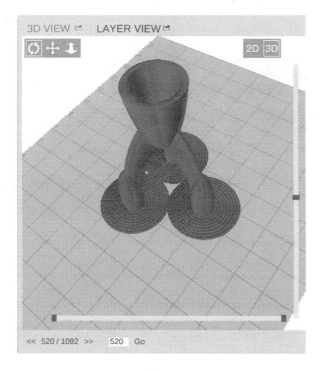

Figure 8-1. *MatterControl's Layer View halfway through the print*

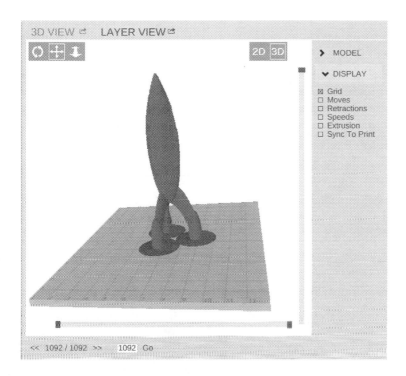

Figure 0-2. MatterControl's Layer View of the complete print

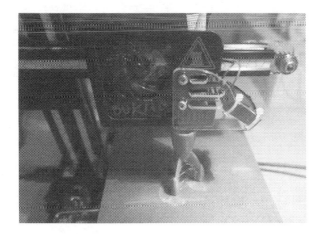

Figure 8-3. The hollow-object print in progress. Note the brim

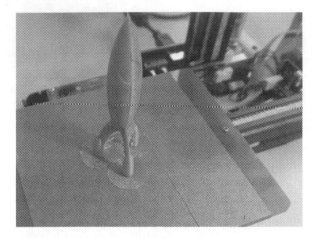

Figure 8-4. *The complete hollow-object print*

In Figure 8-4 you can see a seam along the length of the spaceship. in each layer, there is a small artifact where the extrusion starts and stops along the outer perimeter. When the printer creates infill before starting the next perimeter, the location of these artifacts is randomized, but without infill, they usually line up and create a seam running down the side of the print like that in Figure 8-4.

Printing Vases

Sometimes you may want to print something that looks like a vase, or a bowl—open on the top, but with a closed bottom. You can do that using the Spiral Vase print mode. Go to Settings & Controls ➤ SETTINGS ➤ General ➤ Layers/Surface ➤ Outer Surface – Perimeters and check the Spiral Vase box (in this mode, MatterControl ignores the Fill Density and Top Solid Layers settings, using 0 for both). Note that vase prints should be created as solid objects with a flat top so that they can be hollowed out by this process.

Spiral Vase print settings have advantages and disadvantages. Instead of printing a full layer that is, say, 0.2 mm high, a spiral vase (as the name implies) prints continuously up from the base in a spiral. The object is still sliced into layers, but instead of one big vertical move at the end of the layer, there is a very small move after each horizontal move. As with the hollow print in Figure 8-4, this can create a seam down the side of the print, but is it usually a bit less pronounced. You can see how translucent the vase in Figure 8-5 is; it was printed with silver PLA.

Figure 8-5. *A vase print. Design by Rich Cameron in OpenSCAD*

▓ **Tip**   It is relatively easy to create amazing vases in OpenSCAD (discussed in Chapter 4) using the
`linear_extrude` function. The following line is an OpenSCAD program in its entirety to print a simple vase
(a somewhat less smoothed version of the one in Figure 8-5):

```
linear_extrude(height = 60, twist = 360, scale = .5) translate([10, 0, 0]) circle(30);
```

Figure 8-6 shows another vase print in MatterControl's 3D-View, partway up. It is a good idea to check
your vase print to be sure that nothing went wrong and that there are indeed no infill or top layers.

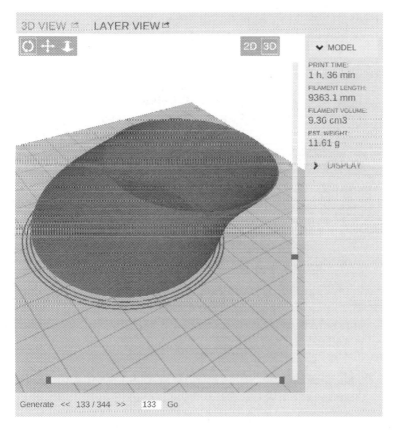

Figure 8-6. *A vase print in MatterControl*

Multiple Extruders

The choice of materials gets more complicated with printers that have more than one extruder because they
can print in more than one color or more than one material at a time. If you are using, say, two colors of PLA,
probably there will not be any problems other than creating the two-color model in the first place. However
if you are using more than one material, it gets a little trickier. In this section, we work through an example of
setting up a dual-extruder print in MatterControl and discuss issues that arise printing in two materials, or
just two colors of one material.

Dual-Extruder Printing with Two Different Materials

Printing in two different materials at the same time can be tricky because you may be printing materials in close proximity that individually would be printed with different platform and extruder temperatures, which may mean that one or the other will not be optimal. Here are some considerations to bear in mind if you embark on a two-material print:

- Which material will (primarily) be present in the first few layers? The bed temperature or platform surface material should generally be set to favor the material that primarily will directly interface with the platform. A raft of one material or the other can solve this problem.

- Are the materials extruded at very different temperatures? If so, you might have to experiment with printer speed to give layers more time to cool before another layer is placed on top.

- Controlling ooze (the nozzle "drooling" a bit when it is hot and filament is left in it) can be a problem in dual-extruder printers. Because each extruder will be sitting around without extruding for about half of the printing time, you may want to use a temperature at the lower end of the range for that plastic to keep the ooze under control. This is all right for PLA, but is a bad idea with ABS because inter-layer adhesion can be compromised by giving you a lower bonding temperature in a print that already has more layer cooling time than normal. When you have Slic3r selected as your slice engine, there is an option to prevent ooze while printing with the other extruder by lowering the temperature of the inactive extruder just enough to keep the plastic from flowing. Note that this can significantly increase print time because the printer has to re-heat the extruders each time it switches (and on some printers, the re-heating may result in more ooze than just leaving the extruder hot).

- MatterControl has a Wipe Shield slicing option for MatterSlice under Multiple Extruders to help catch ooze and prevent it from sticking to your print. You can also create a Wipe Tower that will prime the extruder each layer to make up for the plastic lost to ooze.

- Consider whether the part will be stressed in any particular direction and be cautious about where you place material-to-material interfaces that might be weak spots. If your two materials don't bond well to one another, you may be able to design them to interlock so that they will not pull apart even if they do not stick.

- Think about where the "bottom" of the object should go to minimize support.

- You will need to pick one of the materials to be used as the material to create support structures to be removed later (if you are not using one material exclusively for that). Think about which material will be the easiest to snap off if you use it for support.

- Are the materials likely to stick well to each other? If not, the design of the object may need to take account of that—for example, by having one material run through the other, minimizing the opportunities for the two materials to pull away from each other.

▓ **Tip** A little experimentation with a small test project is probably the best way to test out settings for printing in two dissimilar materials. Dual-extruder prints can take a while to print because the printer has to switch extruders each layer, so it is best to find problems before embarking on a major print.

Using MatterControl with a Dual-Extruder Printer

MatterControl allows you to use a printer with two extruders. There are two distinct examples: printing dissolvable support (discussed in Chapter 7 but expanded upon here) and printing with two colors or two materials. This process is a little tricky, so plan to take a little time to get everything the way you want it with two-extruder prints.

Printing Dissolvable Support

Chapter 7's section "Dissolvable Support Materials" reviews the filaments commonly used for *dissolvable support,* which is support structure printed with a material that can somehow be washed away instead of pried off. You do not have to do anything special to the model per se to use dissolvable support; under Settings & Controls ➤ SETTINGS ➤ General ➤ Support Material ➤ Extruders, you tell the printer which extruder to use for support material. You will also see a setting for Support Interface Extruder.

░ **Tip**   If you are using a dissolvable support material that is expensive, you can use your regular material for support material and just have the support material interface extruder set to the extruder with the dissolvable material. Then just a thin interface layer connecting the object to its support will be made of the dissolvable material, rather than the entire support structure.

Two-Color or Two-Material Prints

As mentioned, dual-extruder printers allow you to print objects in two colors or materials. It is still a little complicated, though. First, you need to create the STL files for each of the extruders separately, so that you can assign each one to an extruder. In the example here, we will be printing a red heart pendant with a yellow star and yellow exclamation point. This entire object was created in Tinkercad, with the exclamation point, star, and heart all in the same file.

To create a two-color object, we needed to create two separate STL files. To create the first one, we turned the heart/pendant hook into a "hole" in Tinkercad, subtracted it from the merged item, and saved that much into what we will call STL number 1.

Then, to make the second STL, we undid the merging, turned the heart/pendant back into a regular object, and deleted the star and exclamation point so that we could export just that part as STL number 2. Once we had the two files, we imported one of the parts into MatterControl with the +Add button and selected a printer with dual extruders. You will see the results in upcoming figures.

We will now describe the general process you will need to use to print a file like this one and illustrate it with our heart pendant. The directions that follow assume you have two STL files that were created with a process similar to that we just described for our heart pendant- that is, two STLs created in a way that maintains the same coordinate system across the two files.

░ **Tip**   If you are using a printer with two extruders as we are describing here, you will need to enter your manufacturer's offset values, unless they come in with the printer settings prebuilt into MatterControl for your printer. The offset is the distance between the two extruder heads in x and y. In a pinch, you could measure from the center of one nozzle to the center of the other nozzle, but this is difficult to do and your manufacturer should have given you either a number or a means of determining the number from a print. You can specify your settings for two extruders under Settings & Controls ➤ SETTINGS ➤ Printer ➤ Extruder.

To print a dual-extruder print, select one of your two STL files by clicking on it in the queue. Next insert the other file by selecting Insert below the 3D View and then picking the other STL. This process adds the second STL to the build plate and allows editing mode so that the parts can be arranged on the build platform. Next, click the Material tab on the right and select each STL in turn and assign one of the extruders. (You might have to use Ungroup and then select with the icon of a finger on a button (upper left)—see Figure 8-8. Clicking Align at the bottom of the 3D View window returns the objects to the correct positions relative to one another.)

▓ **Note** Check to see which extruder is Extruder 1 and which is Extruder 2 on your machine—it may not be the way you would assume.

Under Settings & Controls ➤ SETTINGS ➤ General ➤ Multiple Extruders ➤ Extruder Change, you may want to change the Wipe Shield Distance and Wipe Tower Size variables (both features are disabled if set to 0). The Wipe Shield is like a skirt drawn around the print, but all the way up the print. It allows the extruders to wipe off between colors so that there is less drooling from one color into another. The Wipe Tower is a square printed away from the rest of the print to help prime each extruder before it begins printing to make up for any plastic that has been lost as ooze, which also serves to wipe the nozzle at that point. You can experiment with your printer to see the minimal values that work.

The heart and star pendant shown in Figures 8-7 through 8-11 was printed with a Wipe Shield Distance of 2 mm and a Wipe Tower Size of 15 mm.

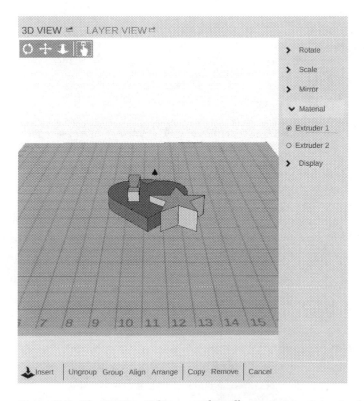

Figure 8-7. *The 3D View Edit screen that allows you to assign extruders to each of the two STL files brought in for the print*

Once you have that set, click Generate in the 3D View window to generate layers and print as usual. Figure 8-8 shows the difference between Hiding Offsets or not. Figures 8-9 shows a simulation of the whole print in Layer View and 8-10 shows the actual print, on a Deezmaker Bukobot Duo, of our heart pendant. The square is the wipe tower. You can see the wipe shield on the platform (it's a little messy, but that is part of the point of its existence).

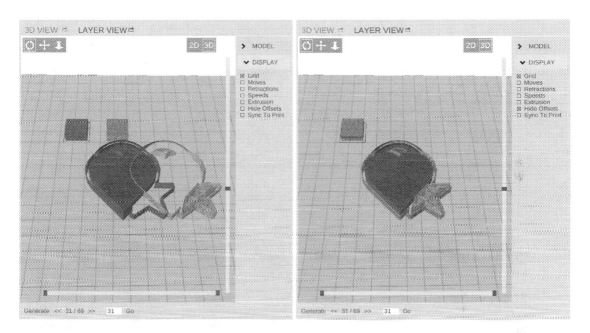

Figure 8-8. *The Layer View allows you to see the print with the extruder offsets shown as if the actual print heads were in the same place (left) and accounted for assuming the offsets you put into the software are correct (right)*

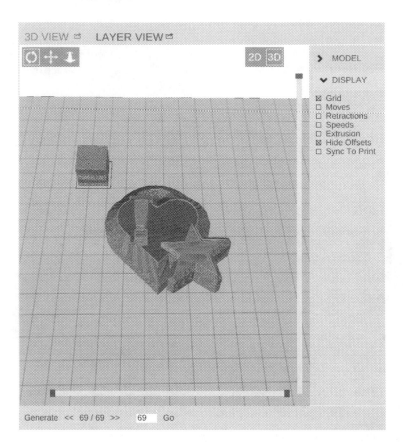

Figure 8-9. Simulated (Layer view) duo print

▥ **Note** By and large, dual extruder-prints take a lot longer than the same print with one extruder, due to the switching and wiping that takes place. As of this writing, only one extruder at a time is in use with consumer printers that we are aware of.

The wipe tower can get a little uneven and get knocked off near the end; that happened with this print about two layers from the end, after the photo in Figure 8-10 was taken. If that happens near the end of a long print, you can let the print finish just drooling over where the wipe tower was as long as the wipe tower wound up somewhere out of the way.

Figure 8-10. *The nearly completed print on the platform with the wipe shield and wipe tower*

Note that the wipe shield in Figure 8-10 curves around the print and does not go straight up. Figure 8-11 shows the completed dual print with the wipe shield and tower removed.

Figure 8-11. *The final product*

Summary

In this chapter you learned how to print a hollow object, a vase, and a two-extruder print. All these require a slightly different thought process in the setup phase of the 3D printing process. In the case of a dual-extruder print, you may need to do some experimenting to get the settings just right for your printer so that you can either print dissolvable support or two-material prints.

PART III

■ ■ ■

Your Printer at Work

This final part of the book covers how to use your printer for various applications. Chapter 9 goes over how MatterControl can help you stay organized with its file and settings management capabilities.

Chapter 10 gives some more examples of the end-to-end flow of using MatterControl to slice a file and control a printer.

Chapter 11 gets into MatterControl's plugin capabilities and the currently available plugins.

And finally, Chapter 12 introduces what you can do to make your prints better by post-processing them (and by diagnosing and correcting some common problems).

CHAPTER 9

■ ■ ■

File and Settings Management, and the Touch Tablet

MatterControl provides some functionality to help you manage your files and your printer settings. The software allows you to slice files and keep them ready to print in the queue, or to deposit them in a searchable library. A powerful settings-management system also makes it easier to keep track of different settings for different types of print. This chapter also talks about the MatterControl Touch tablet and how to use it.

File Management: The Queue

When you bring an STL or G-code file into MatterControl by clicking the Add button, it will be added to the queue. STL files generate a 3D View of the object by default, and G-code files generate a 2D Layer view. The queue will persist if you close down MatterControl and restart it (on the same computer).

If you select a file in the queue by clicking it, you can then export the file, copy it, or send it to the library (see Figure 9-1). Hovering the mouse pointer over a queue entry will give you options to View or Remove the file. If you click Edit, you can use the check boxes to delete multiple files at once or to send them all to the library. Clicking Done gets you back to the queue.

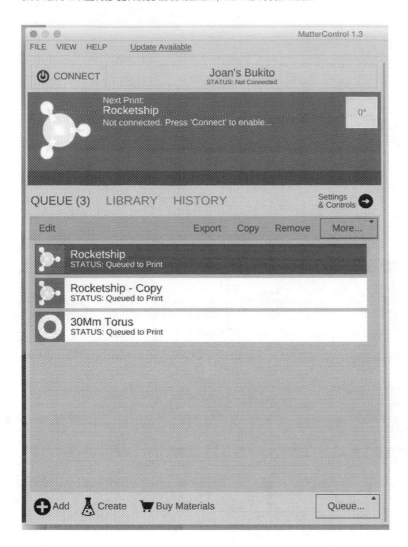

Figure 9-1. *The Queue*

The MatterControl Library

MatterControl's local library is a searchable archive of files (STL, AMF, or G-code) that resides on your computer. It also has a cloud library (which requires that you have a MatterControl account). To get into the library, click LIBRARY to get the screen shown in Figure 9-2. The two libraries are distinct, and as of this writing, moving files directly from one to the other is not possible.

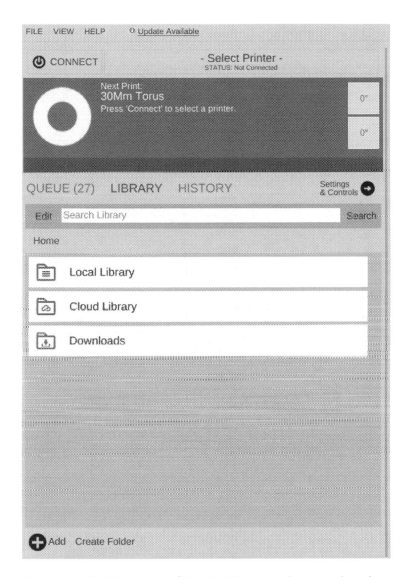

Figure 9-2. *The Library view. (Note that this screen shot was taken after many more files were added to the queue after the shot shown in Figure 9-1.)*

To take a file from the queue into the *local* library, select the appropriate library folder (in the screen with the queue visible) and click More ➤ Add to Library. MatterHackers is developing the cloud library as this books goes to press; the process of putting something into the *cloud* library will be to open cloud library and click +Add to select a file from your computer's file system.

To export a file from the queue or run it, click Edit on the screen that shows the Library, with Library selected (see Figure 9-3), and then select the file with the check box on the left. You can then use the Export, Edit, Remove, Rename, or Add to Queue functions.

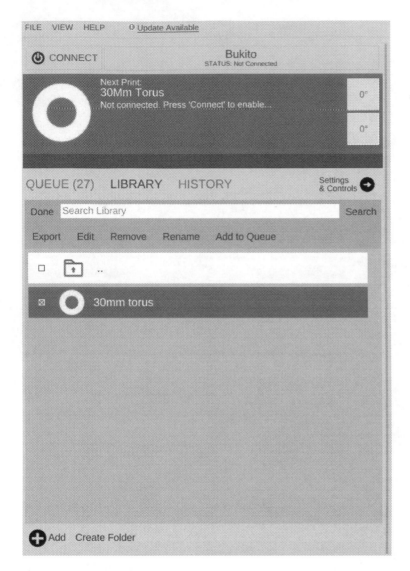

Figure 9-3. *The local library*

Settings Management: Pre-sets

We talked about pre-sets a bit in Chapter 5's section "Changing the Slice Engine Settings." We did not talk a lot there, though, about why you might want to use pre-sets and when they might particularly come in handy. MatterControl's pre-sets are among its most powerful features. Other slicing programs break up slicing settings into categories, and some (like Slic3r) have the ability to manage profiles for different categories independently so that you can mix and match, but sometimes there are printing procedures that require changing settings from multiple categories.

For example, if you are printing extremely fine quality, you will want to print thinner layers and possibly print slower, but you may also want to lower the temperature to account for the fact that less plastic is flowing. On the flip side, for a coarse, fast print, you want to increase the layer thickness (under General settings), but you may also want to increase the temperature (under Filament settings), and maybe even lie to the slicer about your nozzle diameter (under Printer settings) so that it will produce wider extrusions. MatterControl allows you to create one package of settings that will do all of this.

At any time, you can have two pre-sets selected. The first is for Quality, which can specify things like layer height, or if you prefer, you can use it to change settings for a raft, along with the settings that control adhesion of the print to the raft or platform, or you can have a pre-set for vase mode prints.

The second set of pre-set options is called Material. These pre-sets are intended to allow you to adjust settings for different types of filament, such as PLA, ABS, or a soluble support material. If you have multiple extruders, you will be presented with Material pre-sets for each extruder so that you can adjust the settings for each independently. If both the Quality and Material pre-sets modify the same setting, the Material setting takes precedence.

When you view slicing settings while a pre-set is active, you can see which settings are being modified by which pre-sets, and MatterControl gives you the option to edit the pre-set if you hover your mouse pointer over the modified setting (see Figure 9-4).

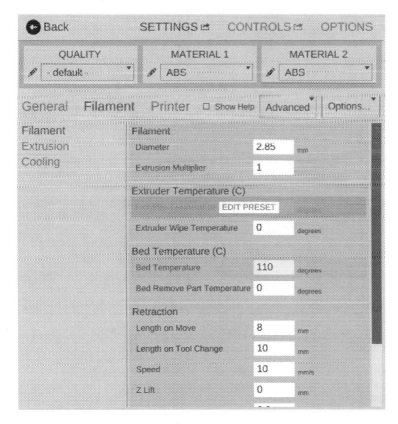

Figure 9-4. *Pre-set overriding previous filament settings*

The MatterControl Touch Tablet

The MatterControl Touch tablet (pictured back in Figure 2-7) is an Android-powered tablet computer that allows you to use MatterControl away from a full-blown laptop or desktop computer. It is preloaded with MatterControl and automatically checks for available software updates. It has a camera and the ability to use a wifi network.

To use the Touch, you need to set it up on a wifi network, plug it into a power outlet, and plug it into a 3D printer. The MatterControl Touch tablet has a microSD card slot that can be used to transfer both STL or G-code files and .slice files produced by exporting a profile or pre-set from MatterControl. You can export a profile or .slice file for each pre-set on your laptop/desktop, put it on an SD card, move that card to the tablet, and import it.

Creating a MatterHackers Account

To move files onto the Touch via a network connection, you need to have a MatterHackers account. To create an account, click the "(sign in)" area in the upper right of the MatterControl window. Follow the directions from the Create An Account link. You will have to sign in with your account on both the tablet and the desktop version of MatterControl in order to link the two.

Running a Printer from a Touch

Let's say you are on a laptop computer and you want to use the Touch to run your print. If the Touch is attached to a printer, when you click More ➤ Send from the laptop's screen displaying the MatterControl queue, you select the name of the printer. The file goes (wirelessly) to the Touch that has that printer selected. The advantage, beyond avoiding tying up a laptop for hours, is that the Touch is dedicated to the print and is less likely to glitch than a laptop would be (and thus less likely to interrupt a print).

MatterControl gives you the option of slicing a file on the laptop/desktop machine and then sending it over to the Touch, or alternatively slicing it on the Touch itself. For very large files, we recommend slicing on a more powerful machine than the Touch and sending it over, although if your network is slow your tradeoffs may be different.

The Camera

The Touch tablet has a camera that can be arranged to watch your printer with a picture that is updated about every two minutes. To turn it on, go to the Options page of the Touch and under Camera Monitoring select ON (and use Preview to figure out the correct view).

To watch the camera remotely, on your laptop or desktop (as opposed to on the Touch) under Options ➤ Cloud Settings ➤ Cloud Monitoring, click ENABLE (if it is disabled). Click View Status to bring up a web page. On that web page, click Dashboard to bring up a page like that shown in Figure 9-5.

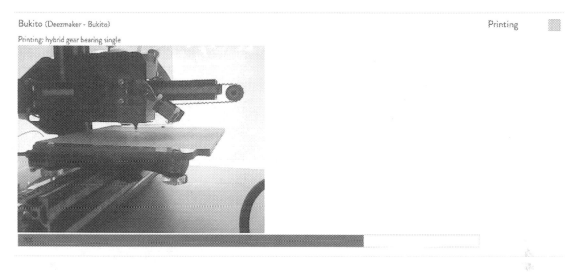

Figure 9-5. The in-process picture

The picture updates infrequently but it can give you an idea of whether things are going generally okay. By default, though, it does not take a picture at the end of the print. To have a picture at the end sent to you, on the Touch under Options ➤ Cloud Settings ➤ Notification Settings, select your desired notification and on the bottom be sure to click the box to include a photo, too. The desktop MatterControl does not give you this option.

▨ **Tip** You can get a MatterControl Touch tablet from the MatterHackers.com store.

Summary

This chapter covered the file and settings-management functions of MatterControl. In addition to the MatterContol software tools, this chapter discussed the MatterControl Touch, a tablet computer that can act as a dedicated 3D-printer host, connecting via wifi to other computers you may be using to generate files. We discussed the workflow using the tablet and the currently available features of the tablet.

■ ■ ■

CHAPTER 10

Case Studies and Classroom Tips

The chapters to this point have covered a lot of information about how to set up the MatterControl software, create a 3D model, slice it, and print it in your chosen material. Now we will walk through a few case studies to show you how to think about particular design problems, how to make an object as simple to print as possible, and how to anticipate issues you may have to deal with during the print. If you are already a sophisticated user and want tips and tricks, the later examples on fine detail will help you there.

The material in this chapter to a degree echoes the material in Chapters 4 through 7. We do not explicitly refer back to those chapters by and large, but we apply that material here and in some cases expand upon it a bit for a particular case. The goal of this chapter is to give you some intuition about good practices so that you can, over time, learn all the details without being overwhelmed. Refer back to the section "3D Printing Design Rules" in Chapter 5, too, for general principles.

■ **Tip** This chapter gives you some typical settings to use and lays out what we think about when confronted with a particular printing scenario. In general, the best strategy is to keep the model as simple as possible and try out changing slicing settings or orientations one at a time. A good open source 3D printer gives you a lot of flexibility in the settings you will use, but it also can have a long learning curve. Find some ways of keeping track of what does and does not work (Joan likes to keep a small hardbound notebook for the purpose) and keep your presets named and stored in some systematic way so that you can reproduce success.

We use screenshots from MatterControl and settings appropriate for a typical, small, open source 3D printer: a Deezmaker Bukito using PLA. The details of a given machine will be different, but by walking through our thought process here for a few typical, easy cases and some sophisticated ones, you will develop some intuition to learn the details in an orderly way as you go. Some special cases (a vase print, hollow objects, and objects made with a dual-extruder printer) are covered in Chapter 8 and we do not return to those here. This chapter focuses on common issues and tries to make some suggestions for print design success.

This chapter also reports on some experiences we have had while coaching teachers and school staff as they in turn figured out how to use 3D printing in their classroom projects. We are grateful to the Windward School teachers, staff, and administration for their support of these efforts, and to the very creative students who designed and made some of the objects you will see later on in the chapter.

Simple Print

For your first attempt at 3D printing, try printing a simple object. That's easy to say, but how do you know that an object *is* "simple"? To get started, imagine how the object might print up from the build platform:

- Does the object have a big flat area that can be its base on the platform?

- If you put the object down on that flat area, can you print it without encountering any steep overhangs?

- Did you avoid having the bottoms of any features floating in mid-air?

- Are there thin walls or little protrusions less than 2 to 3 mm across? If so, then this model is *not* simple; see the section "Printing Fine Detail" later in this chapter.

A yes answer to the first three questions means that the object does not need support. Even if a surface is very smooth and rises gradually (like a sphere) if it has a tiny contact area with the platform, it will need support and/or a raft or brim that typically will be hard to get off. If any features are hanging down from an otherwise smooth bottom of the print, they will need to be supported.

Finally, sometimes an object's detail is just too fine to reproduce with a consumer-level 3D printer, although thinking about the orientation of the layers versus the detail can squeeze out a bit more performance, like the printing Braille example later in this chapter.

▨ **Note**   An object that *appears* simple (like a big sphere, about which more in a little bit) is not necessarily a simple object to print. Conversely, something that looks very complex might actually not be all that bad to print if you can find a way to avoid the preceding list of issues.

For our simple print example, Joan developed a little pendant in Tinkercad showing stars poking out from behind a cloud (Figure 10-1). This was created by merging together half-spheres to create the cloud, then adding a ring and stars. Half-spheres and stars are prefabricated drag and drop primitives in Tinkercad, and the ring was made using one of Tinkercad's shape generators that allows you to specify the shape of the cross-section and a few other parameters, so nothing should have gone wrong.

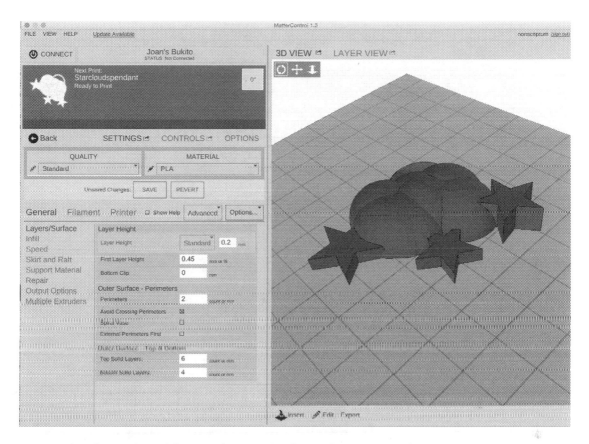

Figure 10-1. *The simple model settings for Layers/Surface and its 3D View before slicing*

Steps in MatterControl for the Simple Model

Running a model like this requires checking that several settings are appropriate, once you have selected a printer and added a file to the queue. Note that we usually recommend viewing the Advanced SETTINGS , but what follows is also available in the Basic version.

- Go to Settings & Controls ➤ Settings ➤ Layers/Surface and see whether the settings are at the resolution you want. The ones in Figure 10-1 are reasonable for many prints.

- Go to Settings & Controls ➤ Settings ➤ Skirt and Raft and be sure that Create Raft is unchecked (Figure 10-2).

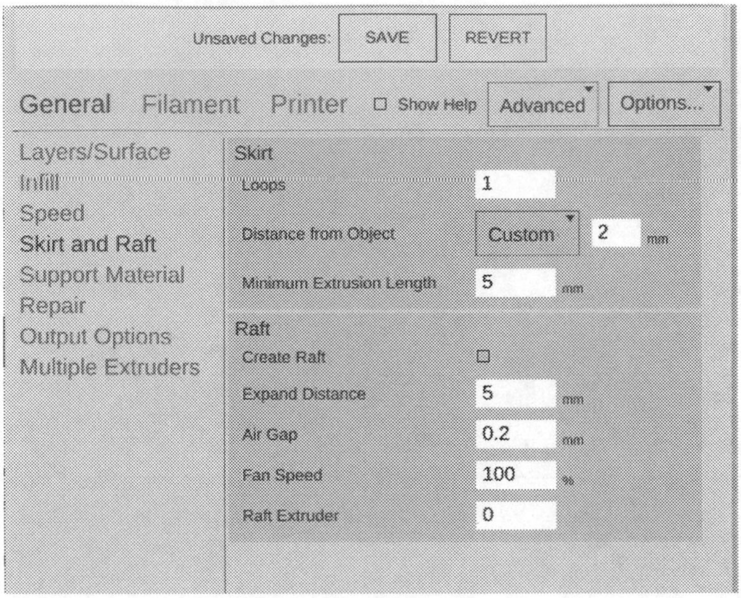

Figure 10-2. *The simple model settings for Skirt and Raft*

- Make sure that "Generate Support Material" is unchecked by going to Settings & Controls ➤ Settings ➤ Support. (Depending on the model and on your other settings, slicing with support enabled for objects that don't need it may result in the slicing engine trying to create support structures that are not really needed.) Then click Layer View and Generate to slice the file. If you then select the 3D View and drag the slider to see the whole print, you will see a screen like that in Figure 10-3.

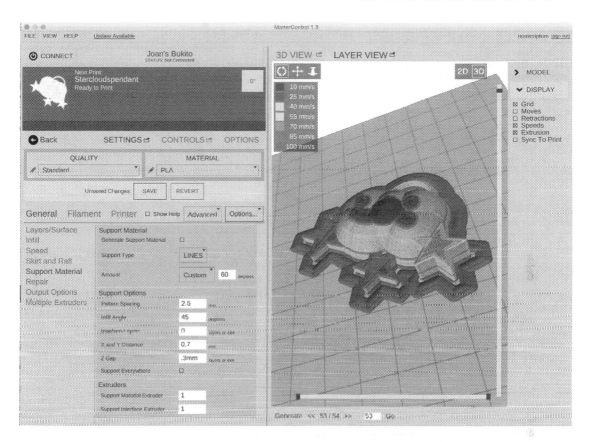

Figure 10-3. *The Support Material settings for the simple model, and its Layer View showing speeds and the skirt*

At this point you should look at your print in the Layer View and see if anything seems to be amiss (more about what to look for is coming up in the next section). If everything looks fine, you can run it directly on your printer if the printer is connected to your computer via USB. Alternatively, go back to the 3D View, click Export, and save the file as G-code. You can move it to your printer on an SD card or to your MatterControl Touch tablet (see Chapter 9). Or you can run it directly on your printer if it is connected to your computer via USB.

Figure 10-4 shows the print partway through, and Figures 10-5 and 10-6 show the finished print on the printer and after it has been taken off the printer. Things do not always go this smoothly, though, even for an experienced user. In the next section we talk about the things that went wrong with this model and how we fixed them. Over time you will gain experience in which things are easiest to catch in your modeling software of choice and which are easier to see in MatterControl. In any case, assume that you will need to do a bit of iterating with many of your models.

Figure 10-4. The clouds and stars print partway through, showing the skirt and infill

Figure 10-5. The clouds and stars print as it finished on the printer

Figure 10-6. The clouds and stars print close up—compare with Figure 10-3 preview

Typical Model Mistakes and How to Avoid Them

Even the simplest model can surprise you when you bring it into MatterControl and go to slice it. Consider the components of the model in Figure 10-1. The first time Joan took the model through the process we just described, she took a look at the Layer View and noticed that the first layer only consisted of a circular area, whereas she expected something like Figure 10-7 for the first layer. A little thought revealed that one of the half-circles was poking down more than the others. A trip back to Tinkercad was required to fix that one.

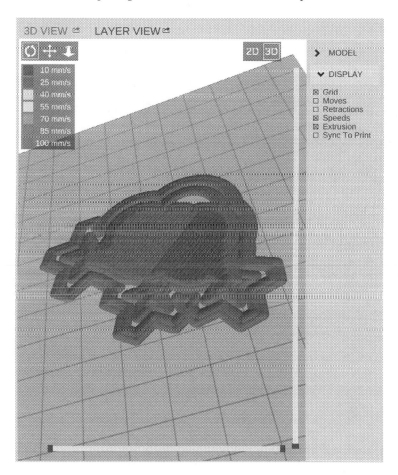

Figure 10-7. *The simple model first layer (simulated in MatterControl) as it should appear*

A subtler error remained, though. A first print had a very ragged arc on top. It turned out that the "ring" in Tindercad tapers to a point on the ends of the ring. Joan had to cut the ring across its diameter to get a finite-width bottom for the arc. She also thickened that piece a little.

This type of problem can often be found by walking through the layers in the 3D Layer View of MatterControl. Even as experienced users, we prevent failed prints all the time this way. The Display menu on the right side of the Layer View panel allows you to show when the print head is moving (and not extruding) or when it is retracting (pulling filament back in when traveling across empty areas). Sometimes turning these display features on or off can help you debug what is going on with a print.

It is also easy to forget to turn support on or off, or to leave a raft in place when you did not want one. Walking through the simulated print saves time, filament, and frustration. 3D printers do not, for the most part, prevent any of this type of failure, and it is up to the user to be alert and anticipate what might go wrong.

Sometimes there is nothing in the Layer View. This means that perhaps your model may not have a physically possible geometry—it may be a one-sided cup with no modeled interior, for example. Chapter 4 talks about how to handle those problems.

You may have noticed that the first layer print in Figure 10-7 prints at a very slow speed. Rich believes in having very slow first layer speeds to maximize the chance that a print will stick to the bed. In Figure 10-3 you can see that the print slows down at the top, too. In that case, it is because each layer is so small that the printer slows down to allow each layer to cool before the next starts. These adjustments are somewhat automatic (in that your printer manufacturer will suggest speeds), but you can adjust them in SETTINGS (with the Advanced option selected) ➤ General ➤ Speed; and Filament ➤ Cooling ➤ Cooling Thresholds.

Printing with Support

The simplest object to print that may or may not require support is a sphere. A printer can handle some degree of overhang, but how much you can get away with depends a little on the printer, the material, and how the slicing software optimizes the print. In this section we will print a 30 mm diameter sphere with and without support. Sometimes it is unambiguous that you will need support if a part is sticking out. Imagine printing a statue of someone pointing at you accusingly, for example; when the printer went to print her arm, the plastic would just fall into space if there were no support. However, many situations are not so clear-cut. This section looks at a simple case of trying the two options. Figure 10-8 is the Layer View of a sphere without support, and Figure 10-9 is the same view of one with support. In Figure 10-9 you can see the options chosen to generate the support. Figure 10-10 shows the completed print of the unsupported sphere; Figure 10-11 shows the supported one.

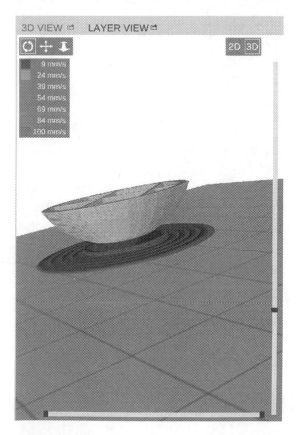

Figure 10-8. *The Layer View of a sphere without support*

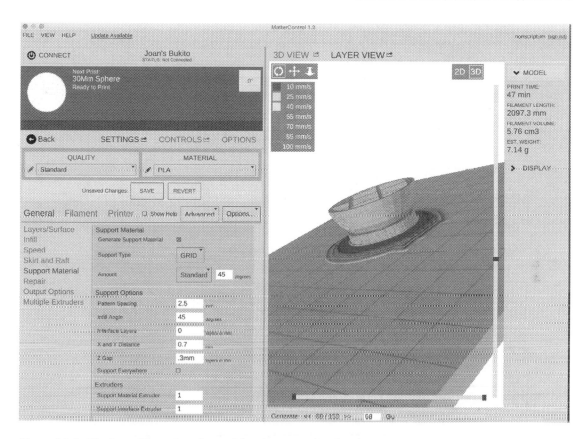

Figure 10-9. *The Layer View of a sphere without support, showing the support options in use*

Figure 10-10. *Completed unsupported sphere*

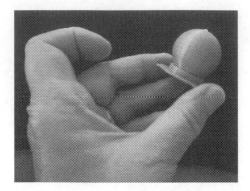

Figure 10-11. *Completed supported sphere, with support still on it*

In Figure 10-12 you can see the final result: the unsupported print next to the supported print with the support removed. The unsupported one has a bit of irregular "drool" on it, whereas the supported one has some residual support. Chapter 12 talks about post-processing to make this a little better, but the bottom line is that either choice has some negatives. Usually, we try to push as far as we can to avoid support, and sometimes we start a print to see if it will make it and just start over if not.

Figure 10-12. *Completed somewhat cleaned-up spheres, without support (L) and with (R)*

Printing Fine Details

Fine features can be difficult to print. A 3D printer extrudes a string of plastic about half a millimeter wide (exactly how wide depends on your slicing settings and the size of your nozzle), and the outer surface on each layer has to be a closed loop. That means that the features in each 2D slice need to be at least 1 mm across to be reproduced accurately. When features are smaller than that, the slicer may try to find a way to produce them anyway, sometimes with unpredictable results. More often, though, the slicing program will drop these small features from the print entirely.

Text on a Print

For some shapes, such as the edge of a knife blade, the loss of the excessively thin portion may still allow the print to represent the overall shape reasonably well. For others, like loose clothing on a model of a person, an area of the model that is too thin may result in a print with an unexpected hole. Having features that are missing due to being too thin is especially common and problematic when trying to print characters (text, numbers, or even Braille dots) on a 3D object.

There are, however, steps you can take to mitigate these problems. The first and most obvious is to avoid thin features in your model. In the case of text, this means using a font that does not have thin features. Bold, blocky, sans-serif typefaces are generally easiest to print, and larger characters are easier to print than smaller ones. This is why tools like TinkerCAD and MatterControl's "Text Creator" plugin, discussed in Chapter 11, use blockier typefaces.

Effects of Print Orientation

You can also widen the cross-section of a feature by not printing that feature vertically. A horizontal feature can be as thin as a single layer, and when letters protrude from a vertical wall, their horizontal lines can be much thinner than when those same features can be in letters that are printed facing up. Small features, like the dot on the letter *i* or those that make up Braille text will also be damaged more easily when they are printed facing up. When these features are on the side of a print, they are just a slight deviation of a straight line in the perimeter of a layer, but when printed on top, these features are on a separate layer from the surface they are printed on, with only a small area to adhere to the previous layer. These features will be relatively easy to break off.

Another option for printing characters is to make ones that do not protrude from the surface at all, but are instead cut into the surface. When letters are set into the surface, the features that need to be printed are not the lines that make up the letters, but the space around those lines. The printer can create spaces between features that are much smaller than the features themselves. This is also the only practical way to create text on the bottom of print. This does not work for Braille text, which is required to be poking out of the surface, but can be an interesting alternative otherwise.

Figure 10-13 shows the layout of an experiment printing a flat plate with block text, a cursive font, and some Braille dots horizontally and vertically. (The text was on the outside of the pair of vertical plates to minimize stringing on the text.) We also printed a similar pair of plates for recessed text to see the difference.

Figure 10-13. *The four blocks on the printer. The ones that are flat on the platform are the ones we will refer to in the text as "horizontal"*

Figure 10-14 shows the resulting two vertically oriented plates and two horizontally oriented plates. The vertically printed plates (which have horizontally printed text) appear darker, with 0.1 mm layer height letting us get away with printing most of the text. This was printed on a Bukito with a 0.5 mm nozzle using Prototype Supply PLA. Figure 10-15 is a closeup of the vertically printed block (characters printed horizontally and protruding).

Figure 10-14. *As-printed four blocks. Top two were printed with the surface vertical; the bottom two were printed flat on the platform. Protruding text is on the left, recessed on the right*

Figure 10-15. *Closeup of the vertically printed (one side on the platform when printed) protruding text block*

■ **Note** Printing many small, fine features like letters or Braille dots on the horizontal surface of a block may result in excessive retraction. This can cause strings of plastic between features, and can even make your extruder more likely to jam (which usually results in a failed print).

Unusual Slicing: The Quick-Print Gear Bearing

Some advanced prints use models that are designed to print with non-standard slicing settings. These settings produce printed shapes that intentionally will not match the digital preview in MatterControl. These models are designed to interact with special slicing settings to produce shapes that would be difficult to produce any other way. You saw a simple example of this in Chapter 8 when we described how to print a vase using a model that actually was not open and vase-shaped, but could be interpreted that way.

A more extreme example is Rich's planetary gear bearings, designed to print quickly using single-wall settings, based on a model by Emmett Lalish (see the links for both in Note that follows). The original can take hours to print and often results in gears that are either stuck together or too loose (depending on how well the printer is calibrated), but this version prints in about 15 minutes and allows you to adjust the tolerance between gears in the slicing settings by modifying the thickness of the walls. It does this by inverting Emmett's model so that the model you are printing is the negative space between the gears in the original. The tolerance between gears has been increased to include twice the wall thickness (0.7 mm, in this case) so that when it is printed without infill or top and bottom solid surfaces, the holes in the shape become separate pieces that move freely.

▦ **Note**   If you want to try this yourself, the STL is on the Youmagine database, at www.youmagine.com/
designs/quick-print-gear-bearing. This design is based on Emmett Lalish's gear bearings, available at
www.thingiverse.com/thing:53451.

In order for the pieces to move freely, you also have to make sure that the extruder retracts when crossing the empty space (where there would normally be infill) between the gears. Some slicing engines, such as CuraEngine, do not have this option, so it is almost impossible to print without strings of plastic preventing the gears from turning smoothly. Slic3r has an "Only Retract When Crossing Perimeters" option that you can disable, and MatterSlice operates this way by default. This is a situation where MatterControl's modifier presets (see Chapter 5's section "Changing the Slice Engine Settings") come in handy, because you can create one that will change the necessary settings for this type of print and only use it when slicing the appropriate model.

Figure 10-16 shows the visualized STL file—the area that looks *solid* in this view will be the *empty space* in the print because the printer is just printing the walls of the "solid" space (Figure 10-17 shows the completed print). The first layer and a layer in the middle are shown in Figures 10-18 and 10-19. Figure 10-20 shows the MatterControl pre-set file, which presumes MatterSlice is being used as the slice engine. These were printed in PLA. Notice (in Figure 10-17) how translucently thin the outer wall is.

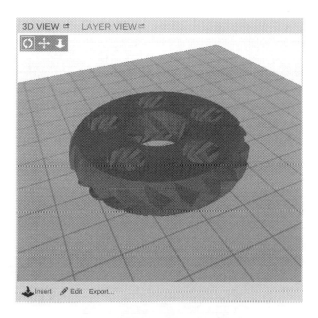

Figure 10-16. *3D View of the STL file (not what the final print looks like, in Figure 10-17!)*

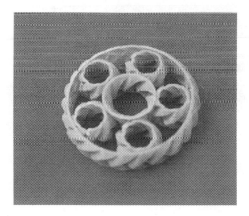

Figure 10-17. *The resulting print of Rich's gear bearing. Note how thin the walls are*

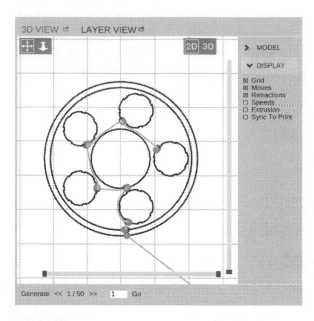

Figure 10-18. *The first layer of the gear bearing (including a skirt)*

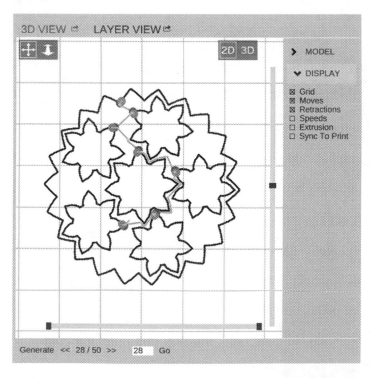

Figure 10-19. *A layer in the middle of the gear bearing skirt (note that the clearances will allow the gear to turn freely)*

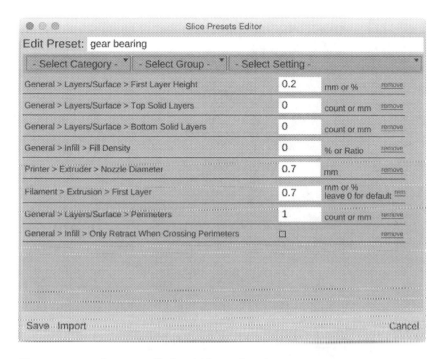

Figure 10-20. *The pre-set file for Rich's gear bearing*

Classroom 3D-Printing Observations

The two of us have been involved in helping teachers learn how to use 3D printing and associated technologies. In particular we have been working with colleagues at the Windward School, in West Los Angeles, trying to make it possible for kids to learn to design their own creations as part of physics and other classes. All the photos in this section are of designs by students from Windward, primarily 7th and 8th graders.

■ **Tip** This section provides a summary of some best practices we have seen ourselves or heard about. More discussion of using these technologies in a classroom is available in our book *The New Shop Class: Getting Started with 3D Printing, Arduino, and Wearable Tech* (Apress, 2015).

Learning 3D Design

By far the commonest software we hear about for classroom use is Tinkercad (`www.tinkercad.com`) for 8th grade or so on up (see Chapter 4 for more). All Autodesk products (of which Tinkercad is the low, web-based end) are, as of this writing, free to educators. Be sure to check the terms of service to see what the restrictions might be. For example, to register themselves for their own Tinkercad account, students need to be at least 13 years old. For students who know how to program a little, OpenSCAD (see Chapter 4) may be a good choice as well. The models in Figures 10-21 through 10-24 were all created in Tinkercad.

Figure 10-21. *Design by an 8th grade physics student at Windward School*

Figure 10-22. *Parts of a carousel design by an 8th grade physics student at Windward School*

Figure 10-23. *Parts from Figure 10-22, assembled (the carousel seats are airplanes)*

Figure 10-24. *Parts of a group-designed chess set, just off the printer, from Windward School 3D-printing elective class*

It is best to develop a bounded problem for the students as part of a regular class, or as an artistic project in 3D printing per se. For example, you might suggest they design a particular object for a purpose, without specifying too many design details. Completely open time tends to result in students surfing the web for something to print. The prints in Figures 10-21, Figure 10-22 (parts), and Figure 10-23 (the parts in Figure 10-22, assembled) were part of a physics class. The chess set in Figure 10-24 was designed collectively by the students in an elective class learning to 3D print.

Once they have a design in mind, introduce design software and give some minimal instruction to get students started. Having them work in teams helps this process. For a first project, consider requiring that the students design something completely themselves, rather than aggegating from online STL sites.

After they have a little time to brainstorm, explain what makes something easy or hard to print (see the section "3D Printing Design Rules" in Chapter 5) and discuss how to avoid overhangs, details that are too small, parts that are not connected to each other, and so on. Give them at least one overnight breather to absorb all that and create a first STL file version of these designs.

Give feedback on these first STL files and make them fix problems themselves if at all possible. Have them learn to fix problems by looking at the 3D View in MatterControl, not by printing and hoping.

You will observe that our suggested workflow implies that you will need a few class periods to get a print or two ready to go. We feel that the iterative testing is an important part of learning and that students capable of learning 3D modeling software should be able to handle making corrections after a while (with a staff member checking things over before printing).

When to Use a 3D Printer

One of the challenges in using the technology is to come up with something that is simple enough to get started, but hard enough to be something that you could not just as easily make from cardboard. The projects in this section were obviously sophisticated for the age of the students, and not easily made out of craft materials. Start easy to build confidence and figure out the system. The classic thing to do is a key chain or nameplate with a student's name on it (see the next chapter's section on printing text). The trick is to not stop there and to keep going to the next level. 3D printers are not the way to go if you need 500 of something the next day. 3D prints take time, typically hours, sometimes a day or more. MatterControl gives a time estimate before you start, but if you are designing a classroom program around 3D printing work, think those issues through carefully.

Overcoming Challenges

Most schools we have talked to have 3D printers supervised by a staff member who also manages queueing. Printers typically are located in a makerspace, robotics lab, prep room, or similar place—not a classroom— for various practical reasons of ventilation, avoiding damage, and so on.

As noted earlier, 3D printers are slow and can be fussy to keep running with the current state of the art. Allow time and resources for school staff to be trained to use the printers. Talk to other users about experiences and try to become part of a community of users. A local hackerspace or makerspace might be a source for collaboration in this area. Also, as noted briefly in Chapter 7's section "Ventilation, Drafts, and Cooling," be sure that any 3D-printer area is adequately ventilated in accordance with the manufacturer's specifications, as well as any other safety requirements your school's policies may require. 3D printers do not like dust and should not be in a room with wood or other dust, plaster, or other fine powder.

One of the bigger challenges is that 3D prints take a while, and that limits the number of prints that can be made. You can alleviate that problem by having students work in teams, by requiring models to be physically small, or by spreading out a project cycle over a long period of time so that different groups need to print on different days. Training older (high school or undergrad) students to help out has worked well in some early-adopter schools.

Summary

This chapter talked you through several case studies, including a very simple print and one that required support (showing some tradeoffs involved in trying to get away without support). We also looked at what to think about when 3D printing fine detail, such as text or Braille. We covered a case in which the 3D model on the screen will, by design, not look like the final product. Finally, we summarized some things to think about when 3D printing in a school environment.

CHAPTER 11

■ ■ ■

MatterControl Plugins

MatterControl has the ability to extend its functions with *plugins,* pieces of code that are loaded at runtime along with the basic MatterControl. If you are a software developer, you can create your own plugins for your use or explore adding them to MatterControl itself. As an open source project, in principle anyone can add to MatterControl. In practice most development is done by MatterHackers, but the code is put out as open source software on Github.

▓ **Tip** If you are interested in developing a plugin yourself, see instructions at `http://wiki.mattercontrol.com/Developing_Plugins` and the repository at `https://github.com/MatterHackers/MatterControlPlugins`. Or contact MatterHackers through its website: `www.matterhackers.com`

Existing Plugins

At the moment there are just two plugins: Text Creator is freely available, and you can try out Image Creator for free, but it requires you to pay for a code to unlock the ability to save and print the output. Both are available from the screen that shows the print queue; click the Create bubbling beaker icon. You will then get a pop-up window like that in Figure 11-1 and you can launch the plugin from there.

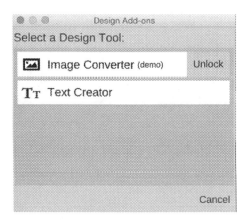

Figure 11-1. *The Plugins pop-up*

Text Creator

The Text Creator plugin, unsurprisingly, allows you to create text to 3D print. To use it, type the text that you want to print at the bottom of the window and click Insert. You can then modify the spacing, size, and height of the letters and decide whether they should have an underline.

By default, the letters are created with an underline that is connected to all of the letters (see Figure 11-2). Without the underline, the letters would be separate pieces and would not form a word after you remove them from the printer's platform. As you can see in Figure 11-3, though, features like the dots over a lowercase *i* or *j* or some punctuation symbols may still be loose. Another option is to decrease the space between letters so that they overlap slightly.

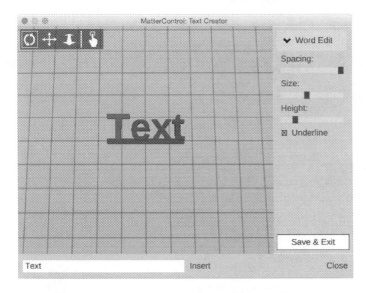

Figure 11-2. *Example of text formatting in Text Creator*

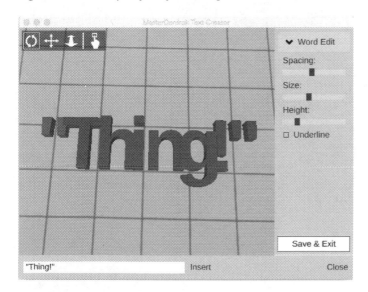

Figure 11-3. *Text in Text Creator showing that some text will still be disconnected*

The Text Creator plugin makes alternating letters a little taller so that you can still see the separation between adjacent letters when you overlap them this way, as you can see in Figure 11-4. Unfortunately, thin letters like *i* may not be wide enough to overlap with adjacent letters, and depending on the shape of the adjacent letters, features like the dot on the *i* may still be disconnected. For these reasons, it is very important to check the shape of the resulting text before printing to make sure the letters will be sufficiently connected—or plan to glue the results onto something else as separate pieces. Figure 11-4 shows a sliced version of Figure 11-3's text.

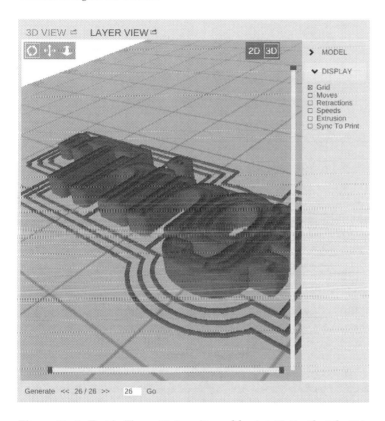

Figure 11-4. *Text in Figure 11-3, as it would print. Notice that the T, i, and g overlap the adjacent letters*

Image Converter

The Image Converter plugin lets you import an image and convert it to a 3D model for printing. If you are hoping that this will allow you to turn a photograph of your dog into a 3D statue, you may be disappointed, because the way it creates 3D models may not be what you expect. A two-dimensional picture does not contain the depth information needed to create a 3D model, nor any information about what the back side of the subject looks like.

Image Converter is not a replacement for a 3D scanner. Instead, it uses the light and dark areas of an image to create a 2D outline and then extrudes it into three dimensions for printing.

You open the Image Converter plugin the same way you got to the Text Creator plugin. Once there, click Add Image and find the picture you want to print. The first thing you want to do is open the Edit Outline section and find the right threshold value to create the outline that you want (see Figure 11-5). In MatterControl itself and in the digital versions of this book, you will see those boundaries in red. They are there in Figure 11-5, but may be difficult to see in greyscale versions of the print book.

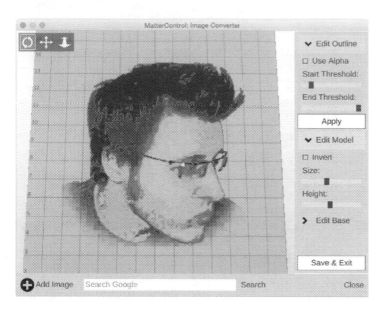

Figure 11-5. *Using the Edit Outline function to create the piece that will be (virtually) extruded*

▓ **Tip**   Image Creator lets you do things like replace the Text Creator with something that will allow you to use custom fonts, create a solid piece from a silhouette image, or turn a child's line drawing (which would extrude as an outline, not a solid piece like our examples) into a custom cookie cutter. Use a food-compatible plastic, and don't put it in the dishwasher if you do! You could export the STL file from Image Creator into Tinkercad or another program and add to it, too.

If your image is a PNG file with transparency, you can check the Use Alpha button to use the transparency instead of the color to determine the shape that you create. As with the Text Creator plugin, you can change the size of the shape as well as the height of the print. If Image Converter is using the light part of your image to create a shape and you want to use the dark part instead, you can use the "Invert" check box to switch between the two.

▓ **Tip**   The End Threshold slider (visible in Figure 11-5) establishes the range of values that are considered in the image for line generation. You can use it to finely adjust the line position by increasing or decreasing the pixels that are measured. It is very subtle and will exert a very small influence on the created edge. (You may think it is not doing anything.) This slider comes in handy in a limited range of circumstances—you can try fiddling with it if you are having trouble getting the edge you want.

You can also add a base to your shape (see Figure 11-6). The base can be rectangular or circular, or you can make it follow the outline of your shape (see Figure 11-7). The Size slider here controls how far the base spreads out around your shape, and if you have a several separate pieces in your model, you may be able to use a large outline base to connect them together so that you have a single piece when you remove your print from the platform. As you can see in these two figures, the plugin retains a general outline but does not maintain any detail or contours in the third dimension.

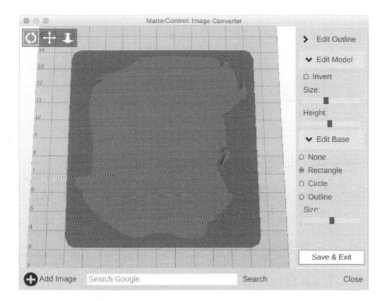

Figure 11-6. *The silhouette from the image in Figure 11-5 with a rectangular base*

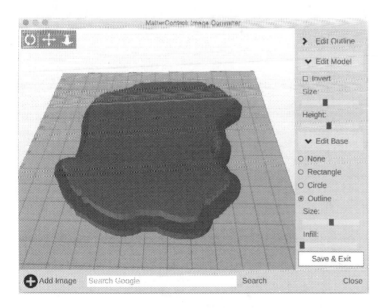

Figure 11-7. *The silhouette from the image in Figure 11-5 with a base that follows the contour of the the figure*

▦ **Note** The example we have shown here is a piece of vector art based on a photogragh. A line drawing is more suitable and will work better, but we wanted to show a more complex case. A line drawing will not require a lot of the adjustments we just described for the photo.

Summary

In this chapter we reviewed the plugin functionality of MatterControl and discussed the two design-oriented examples available as of this writing. These two, Text Creator and Image Converter, are both built into MatterControl, but the latter needs to be unlocked if you want full functionality. We also noted where you can look for more information if you want to contribute a plugin yourself.

CHAPTER 12

■ ■ ■

Troubleshooting and Post-processing

People tend to come into 3D printing either from the software/modeling side or from the electronics hacking or shop class world. Debugging a system with a lot of software involved is a little different from figuring out what is wrong with something that is purely mechanical (or even electronic). And introducing real parts that are being manufactured for the first time creates issues that do not come up in purely virtual software development. You will need to learn the tricks from the community that is less familiar to you, unless you are one of those rare people comfortable in both worlds. This chapter will guide you through some of the common 3D-printing problems that arise and and help you figure out how to resolve them.

In this chapter we talk about how to address some common hardware problems, such as fixing a clogged nozzle. We also look at diagnosing issues related to software settings (such as incorrect retraction settings) that manifest themselves in prints. Many of the issues discussed in this chapter are strongly affected by your printer's design, so take any suggestions here with a grain of salt and read your manufacturer's instructions first before implementing any advice in this chapter.

This chapter also describes how to deal with a model that is either computationally big (an STL file over 50 MB or so) or that, if printed, would be physically too big to fit in a printer's build volume in one pass. Finally, this chapter shows you how to make your prints look a little nicer. A printer will leave behind layer lines, scars from support, or the odd bit of stringing across open areas. We show you how to post-process a model by sanding, painting, dyeing, or chemically smoothing it and offer some tricks for removing support.

Lastly, we summarize some other topics we did not have time to explore in this book and give you some ideas about where you can learn more.

■ **Tip**   When debugging, be very systematic about keeping track of what you have changed and what was different after you changed it, and change the minimum number of things at once. Otherwise, you may go in circles; consider using MatterControl pre-sets (see Chapter 5) to keep track of what groups of settings you have been working with, or a notebook to track the more mechanical aspects.

There are a few common issues that often are caused by a mix of hardware, software, and environmental factors. First, we look at the typical signs of trouble and then cover how to go about analyzing and fixing the problem—or preventing it in the first place. The single commonest problem with a 3D printer is a clogged nozzle, so we show you how to use MatterControl's printer control features to clean out a clog.

How to Unclog a Nozzle

One of the more common problems with a 3D printer is that the printer stops extruding plastic because the extruder nozzle is clogged. The nozzle hole is small and can fairly easily be blocked with debris that was embedded in the filament, dust, or plastic that got too hot and scorched or burned.

▓ **Caution**   These instructions for removing a clog apply generally for any printer with a nozzle rated to the temperatures suggested here. If your nozzle is not rated to 240 degrees C, you should not use this procedure. See Figure 12-1 for an image of the MatterControl Settings & Controls ➤ CONTROLS ➤ Temperature screen, which is where you would set the temperature (see Chapter 6 for more details). Watch the "Actual" temperature for the process that follows, not the "Target" in the box (after you have typed in the target for that stage of the procedure, of course). Note that a printer has to be selected *and* connected (click CONNECT at the top of the screen shown in Figure 12-1) for you to be able to type anything into the Target box.

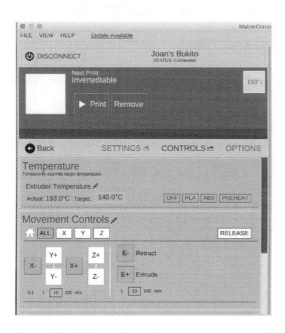

Figure 12-1. *Matter Control temperature screen. (Note that a printer has to be actively connected to set a temperature.)*

Cold Pull

In the past, the only way to get a clog out of a nozzle was to take the entire hot end (nozzle, barrel, and heater block) apart or take it off and put it in a solvent. Because that is not very convenient, and taking the hot end apart can damage it, the *cold-pull* technique was developed. A cold pull starts with inserting filament in the nozzle, just as if you were going to print with the filament, and then pulling the filament back out to pull out any contaminants.

Instead of using the usual extrusion temperature, though, which would melt the filament, the filament is pulled out at a lower temperature—one that is sufficiently warm to allow the plastic to stretch enough to pull away from the sides of the barrel so that it doesn't seize up entirely, but cold enough so that the filament stays in one piece. Usually, any debris in the nozzle will then come out with the filament.

The cold-pull technique works best with printers that have polished-smooth stainless steel nozzle barrels. It also works for nozzles that have a polytetrafluoroethylene (PTFE) internal coating. The cold-pull technique has been successfully done with ABS (cold-pull temperature of about 160–180 C). PLA is much more difficult to work with, but a cold-pull temperature of 80–100 C will sometimes work. Taulman 618 nylon filament (pull temperature of 140 C) is far easier and more reliable to use for this purpose due to its strength, flexibility, and low friction.

To begin, remove as much of the plastic that you've been using as possible. To do this, you can attempt a cold pull with ABS or PLA with the temperatures listed previously. Heat your nozzle to 240 C and push the nylon filament into to nozzle. That temperature will thoroughly melt the nylon, allowing it to get through nozzle. Attempt to extrude the nylon slowly. Most clogs (especially those caused by accumulated dust) will not actually block the nozzle entirely but will be pushed into the nozzle and clog it when the nozzle pressure increases and then float up out of the way when left to sit.

Sometimes you will have a hard clog, usually a solid foreign particle lodged in the nozzle, but this is usually not the case. If not, a slow, pausing extrusion should allow you to purge the old printing material. Once nylon starts coming out of the tip, you can begin cooling your nozzle to the pull temperature. See Chapter 6 for information on manually controlling your printer to extrude some filament manually. Finally, gently but firmly pull the filament out of your printer manually, if your printer mechanism allows it, or by retracting it using MatterControl.

▨ **Note** The temperatures specified in the preceding list are maximum temperatures—temperatures above which the plastic is unlikely to come out solid. For best results, always pull the plastic at the lowest possible temperature, and it may help to cool the nozzle well below this temperature and then continually attempt to pull it as the nozzle heats up again.

Figure 12-2 shows some examples of cold pulls. If you pull the nylon out and the surface is rough, dark, discolored, or has black spots around the sides, this indicates that there is residue of overheated or carbonized, burned plastic in the nozzle. If you see this, you should clip off the end and repeat the process until the nylon comes out smooth, clean, and mostly white. Figure 12-3 shows similar examples of a nozzle that was clogged with overheated plastic, rather than burned plastic.

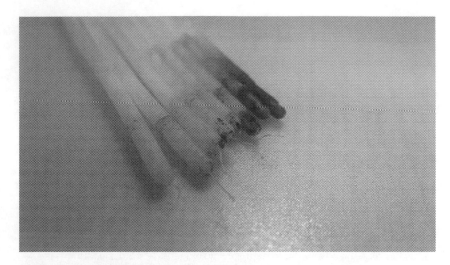

Figure 12-2. *Burned residue on cold-pulled filament*

Figure 12-3. *Nylon with residue of overheated plastic*

■ **Tip**   You may want to do cold pulls from time to time as a preventative measure if your print quality seems to be degrading.

Other Unclogging Techniques

If you are unable to push the nylon in to perform a cold pull, you may have a hard clog. In this case, you will need to carefully poke something into the (hot) nozzle to dislodge whatever is in there. Do not use any kind of drill bit, because that would destroy your nozzle. A bristle from a wire brush works well.

How to Minimize Stringing

Sometimes a print will come off the machine with strings everywhere. Often this means that the retraction settings (Settings & Controls ➤ SETTINGS ➤ Filament ➤ Filament ➤ Retraction) are not correct. When a printer is extruding and has open spaces in a layer, printers pull the filament back so that stringing does not occur.

For direct-drive extruders (where the gear is right next to the nozzle), generally 1-2 mm of retraction is appropriate. A Bowden extruder (with a tube between the drive gear and the nozzle) will usually need a bit more retraction, and you may need to pull back as much as 10 mm if the tube is particularly long. If you have problems with stringing, you may want to increase the retraction length slightly.

Figure 12-4 shows a small inverted table that we will use as a test of retraction on a Bukito printer (which has a short Bowden tube). Figure 12-5 shows the MatterControl screen with a retraction of 2.8 mm; the Layer View shown is a layer when the printer is making the legs of the table. The dots are the starts of retractions, and the thin lines between the legs are the moves of the exruder. (A small amount of random infill is shown too.) Figure 12-6 shows the same thing for no retraction.

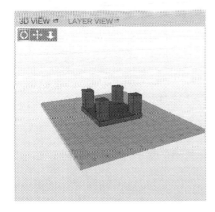

Figure 12-4. *An inverted table to test stringing*

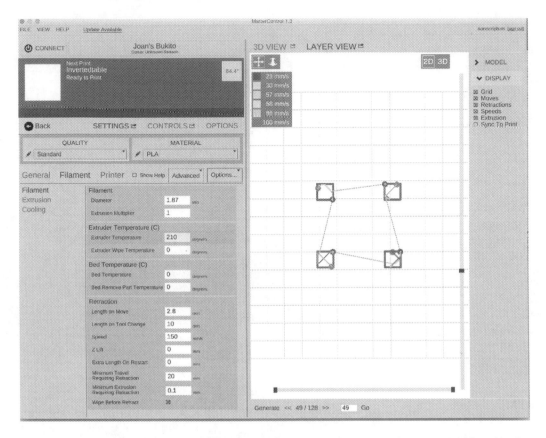

Figure 12-5. *One layer (in the legs part of the print) showing retraction and motion in addition to the print*

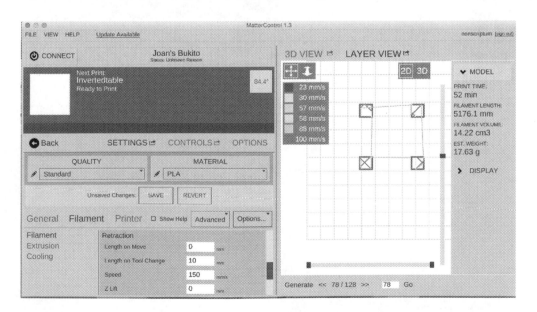

Figure 12-6. *Same model, sliced with different retraction settings*

Finally, Figure 12-7 shows the results of these two as they were printed. Notice there is a lot more stringing on the one with zero retraction. However, there still is some stringing on the print with some retraction; in this particular case, the next thing to try would be to lower the print temperature a bit. Trading off different settings is a matter of experience with your particular printer.

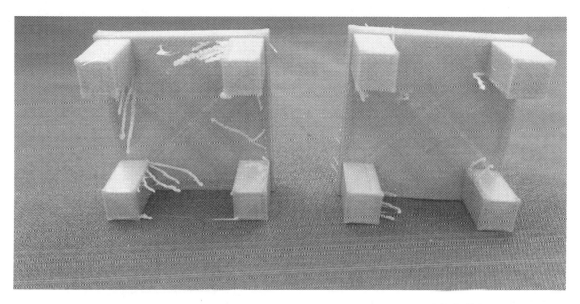

Figure 12-7. *The inverted table, printed as shown in Figure 12-4; put on its side here to show interior. Retraction settings were as shown with no retraction, as in Figure 12-6 (L), and with a modest amount, as in Figure 12-5 (R)*

How to Print Computationally Complex Objects

Sometimes the 3D model of an object is very complex, even if it is specifying a physical print that fits comfortably into the build volume of a printer. Keeping all the detail may be tempting, but the reality is that a consumer-level printer will probably not reproduce detail of a very complex model anyway. If the model is going to be both physically big and very complicated, cutting it (virtually) into pieces and slicing and printing those pieces separately can lower the STL file sizes of the pieces to plausible levels. We talk about that in Chapter 5's section "Avoiding Support By Cutting a Model into Pieces."

▓ **Tip** A very large STL probably has more detail than most printers can reproduce, and it will only serve to make the model more difficult for the slicer and printer to handle. About 50 MB is a practical limit—less if you run the slicing programs on an outdated computer. For a larger file, consider the two techniques discussed in this section.

If you find yourself with an STL file that is too big to work with, you can use the MeshLab program to re-mesh the model with fewer triangles. MeshLab is available at http://meshlab.sourceforge.net. It is a powerful program but can be a little daunting to navigate due to its terminology. Because Meshlab is open source, it can change at any time, but as of this writing the following process will re-mesh an object.

Open MeshLab and import a "mesh" (that is, your STL file) under the File menu. Then click Filters ➤ Remeshing, simplification and construction ➤ Quadratic Edge Collapse Decimation. (You can see the issues here with somewhat non-intuitive menu items for the new user!)

In the dialog box that pops up, you can try cutting the number of surface triangles relative to what the default displays and experiment with the percentage reduction (from no reduction to 100%). A value of 0.5 will cut the number of triangles in half. You can see what you can get away with, based on how the rendering in the program looks. If you have lost an unacceptable amount of detail, don't save the new mesh; import it again and start over. When you like the result, you can export a new STL file.

Alternatively, you can cut the file into pieces as described in Chapter 5 and then glue together the physical pieces after they are built. You will learn about that in the next section.

▓ **Note**   Cutting a file into pieces to reduce the file size (rather than to reduce the dimensional size) will reduce the amount of data that the slicer needs to process, but it can still result in a G-code file with segments so short that they will execute in significantly less time than it takes to transmit and process them. This will result in the firmware slowing down or even pausing between segments, and these unexpected speed changes will result in print artifacts.

Printing from an SD card rather than over USB mitigates these issues, because reading G-code from the SD card is faster than transmitting it over the USB-to-serial connection.

How to Print Physically Big Objects

Consumer-level 3D-printer build areas are for the most part relatively small, because it is a lot harder to manage temperature control and mechanical precision for a large machine. As a result, most consumer printer build areas are under 200 mm or so in any dimension, and many are way under that. This means that if you want to build something bigger than that, you are going to have to cut the object into pieces in software, print the parts, and then somehow construct the final object out of those pieces. For example, if the object is long and skinny, you can cut it into a few objects that you can then arrange on the build platform and print all at the same time. Otherwise, you will have to print the object using multiple runs. In either case, you will need to glue or assemble the piece afterwards.

Objects That Are Too Long for the Build Platform

If you have a long, skinny object that will not fit within the longest build dimension of your printer, first check to see whether it will fit diagonally on the platform. You also want to keep the orientation that will minimize support, so there may be some tradeoffs there. If you are considering printing diagonally in all three dimensions, it may be easier to cut the object in half and later glue two pieces that would both lay flat rather than pick off a lot of support.

If you do need to print a thin but long object (for example, a chopstick), you probably will be able to arrange the pieces on the platform next to each other and print them simultaneously. If, for instance, you were trying to print a tall, skinny tower, you could cut it into several pieces, lay out the pieces on the build platform in one or more groups, and then glue the pieces together.

Objects That Are Too Big in More Than One Dimension

If the object you are trying to print is too big in more than one dimension, you will need to split it along two axes—that is, into at least four pieces, with a lateral slice and a horizontal slice. If any parts require particular precision (if there will be critical joints, for instance), consider where your printer has the highest precision and arrange cuts so that those pieces will fall there. In most cases, the best precision is at the center of the print bed.

▓ **Tip** Even when the full part is too large in two or even three dimensions, it may be possible to divide it into just two or three pieces by judiciously cutting and then orienting the pieces. For example, a letter H that needs to be printed slightly larger than the build platform (in both x and y) can be cut into two halves, each of which may fit diagonally. A pyramid-shaped object that is too tall for the print volume and too wide only in one dimension may be cut into three pieces (the top and two halves of the base). An L-shaped object may be cut into four quadrants, one of which will be empty. Be careful if your printer does not have consistent resolution throughout its build area (most Cartesian printers do).

Chapter 5's section on cutting to avoid supports describes the process of cutting a part in two. To cut into multiple pieces, you follow the same process but cut the piece in half and then cut the halves again (into however many pieces make sense to make the part fit into your printer's build area). The general principles apply. Depending on which program you use to cut up the model, you may be able to slice along several axes at once, or you may have to explicitly make one cut at a time, save the pieces, and then cut them in turn.

▓ **Caution** The techniques discussed in the rest of this chapter are more suited to a "shop" environment (or a chemistry lab) than to a computer lab environment. If you are not used to this type of environment, first work with someone who is experienced to learn safety procedures. Use eye protection and gloves, be sure your space is well ventilated, and follow the chemical manufacturer's instructions.

Gluing the Pieces Together

Once you have printed the pieces, use glue that works on plastics. Cyanoacrylate adhesives ("superglues") work pretty well on PLA and ABS. Nylon is difficult to glue with any adhesive appropriate for home use.

▓ **Caution** Before using any glue, read the manufacturer's instructions and use glues in well-ventilated areas. You may want to try out a particular glue on a few scrap pieces first to be sure that it does not discolor your material. Glues may dissolve pieces a bit, which allows the "welding" process described later in this chapter.

Using an Acetone Slurry

If you are printing in ABS, there's another alternative for adhering pieces to one another (but see the Caution that follows). Acetone will melt ABS and so can be used to weld one piece of ABS to another. Some people put a little bit of acetone in the type of bottle used for nail polish (ones with a small brush) and add the skirt, support material, or other scrap from the print. The acetone will dissolve the scrap into a slurry that will weld the pieces together without melting the edges of the print too much. Or, if precision edges are not important, you can use a drop of acetone to bond the parts together. We talk about using acetone to smooth a print later in this chapter.

▓ **Caution**   Acetone is flammable and volatile. Its vapor is invisible and heavier than air. The vapor can pool if you are in an unventilated area and cause a fire or explosion. Use it in a well-ventilated area without open flames or sparks. Follow the cautions on the manufacturer's label.

Acetone welding only works for acetone-soluble plastics, such as ABS, MABS, and HIPS. Most other 3D-printing filament materials (such as PLA and nylon) are not acetone-soluble. Some PLA formulations (depending on additives) may partially melt, whereas others have been known to warp and crack when exposed to acetone.

▓ **Tip**   When you paint acetone on a part, the acetone evaporates, and you will get a bit of condensation from the air. This can make the surface of the object a bit cloudy. If you are just "welding," then clouding does not matter, but if you are smoothing (described later in this chapter as *chemical smoothing*), it is an issue. Keeping the part slightly warm as it dries helps. If your printer has a heated build platform, you can set your heated platform to 50 degrees C and put the part on it (see the section "Manually Controlling Your Printer" in Chapter 6). Check that the acetone will not damage your platform, though. Never microwave acetone or place it anywhere near a stove; an explosion or fire can result.

Tips on Removing Support

We have talked a lot in this book about removing support, but not a lot about why that is so desirable. In brief, removing support is a pain. If you have a single-extruder printer and therefore have support made from the same material as your object, you need to be careful to avoid damaging the print while removing the support. Needle-nosed pliers work well.

Be sure your tool is strong enough, because otherwise you may snap or bend your tool rather than the support! Small bits of plastic tend to fly everywhere, so protect your eyes. Tweezers are good for the last few bits.

Removing support tends to leave some scarring or a bit of the pattern of the support on the piece. This can be hidden or removed with some of the techniques discussed in the next section.

Sanding, Chemical Smoothing, Painting, and Dyeing

Filament-based 3D printers always produce fine layer lines in printed objects. You can think of them in one of two ways: as inherent in the medium (like brush marks on an oil painting) or as a problem that needs to be resolved. If your application falls into the latter category, this section gives you some ways to get rid of those lines and to color your printed part other than by choosing colored filament. We talk about sanding and chemical smoothing to get rid of layer lines, and then about issues in painting and dyeing finished prints.

Sanding

A bit of sandpaper applied gently to PLA prints can significantly smooth the surface. Just use a piece of sandpaper and sand it by hand—powered sanding is likely to melt the plastic. You will need to start with very coarse sandpaper to remove layer lines and then use progressively finer sandpaper until the surface is as smooth as you want. Wet sanding tends to work best. Figure 12-8 shows four pieces printed from the materials noted in the caption. Rich sanded these (very laboriously!) by hand using many grades of sandpaper, and you can see that it is possible to get a high-gloss finish.

Figure 12-8. *Four pieces that Rich printed and hand-sanded. Top left and front right are PLA. Top right is metal-filled PLA; lower left is wood-filled PLA*

ABS can be sanded but tends to whiten a bit in the process, the same way it bruises when bent. Acetone reverses this discoloration, so sanding can be used in conjunction with acetone smoothing to reduce layer lines while maintaining sharper features that would be rounded off using acetone alone to remove the layer lines. A sanding block may also be useful, depending on the geometry of the part.

Smoothing and Bonding ABS with Acetone

The earlier section "Using an Acetone Slurry" talked about using acetone to weld ABS pieces together. Similarly, a little bit of acetone can be used to smooth an ABS piece using the same techniques (and cautions!) as those described previously. You may need to experiment a bit to see what works.

▓ **Caution**   Do not use acetone on nylon or PLA; nylon is unaffected by acetone. Unfortunately, chemicals that can smooth PLA are too toxic to be used in a home environment.

▓ **Tip**   A lot of smoothing techniques available online use acetone vapor and do-it-yourself devices to create and handle the vapor. We feel that many of these are unwise and/or too hazardous for the intended general audience of this book; therefore, none of these is described in this chapter.

Painting ABS and PLA

You can paint ABS and PLA parts with acrylic paint, like that available in a typical hobby store. If you need a multi-color print and you have a one-extruder printer, painting the object after the fact is a good workaround to produce the colors you need. Recently the epoxy XTC-3D specifically aimed at smoothing 3D prints has come on the market; you can read about it at the manufacturer's website (`www.smooth-on.com/Epoxy-Coatings-XTC/c1397_1429/index.html`) to see if it may be appropriate for your use and environment.

Dyeing Nylon

Although 3D-printed nylon may not look the same as it does in fabric form, it will take up dye in a similar way. Nylon filament typically is white, which makes it easy to dye. People have had good luck with household cloth dyes when dyeing a printed nylon object; check the label on the dye package to be sure that it works on nylon.

Some Final Thoughts

In this book you learned how to use MatterControl and explored the basics of using an open source 3D printer. In the interest of keeping this book focused on the how-to, we have not explored 3D-printing applications or some of the other ways of using a 3D printer. This section summarizes some things you may want to explore next. Some of these are covered in Joan's book *Mastering 3D Printing* (Apress, 2014).

Going from a 3D Print to a Metal Cast

Metal printers are very expensive, but you can use a 3D printer to create a pattern or mold that can then be used in a traditional metal-casting process. The sand-casting process works well using 3D prints as the pattern (a positive mold that is pressed into sand and then removed to make a cavity for casting).

Some experiments have been done using PLA for "lost wax" casting. In this case the print is coated in plaster with strategic holes left in the cast. The cast is heated up, and the PLA runs out, leaving a cavity once again for casting.

Other Printer Technologies

Depending on what you are trying to use, filament-based printing may or may not be the best technique. Resin printers have better resolution, but typically the prints are very small, and the resin is difficult to handle. Powder printers tend to be expensive, and the prints are porous but can be treated to be more durable and smoother.

Printing directly in metal is still expensive but is being used more and more often because machining complex parts costs a lot, too. There is also a lot of interest in biomedical printing (ultimately, in printing body organs!), in printing food, and even in printing concrete.

Applications

For the type of printer described in the book, the early adopters have tended to be hobbyists, then designers, architects and the like, and then gradually schools and the general population. Fundamentally, 3D printing makes it possible to accelerate the process of prototyping hardware the way that home computers allowed people to start creating their own 2D graphics and written documents. The fashion industry is starting to take some tentative steps toward using 3D printing in haute couture. Artists, of course, have many options. Figures 12-9 and 12-10 show a fun kinetic sculpture that Rich designed with many independent pivots; it was printed in one piece. Figure 12-9 shows it on the printer, and in Figure 12-10 it is in motion.

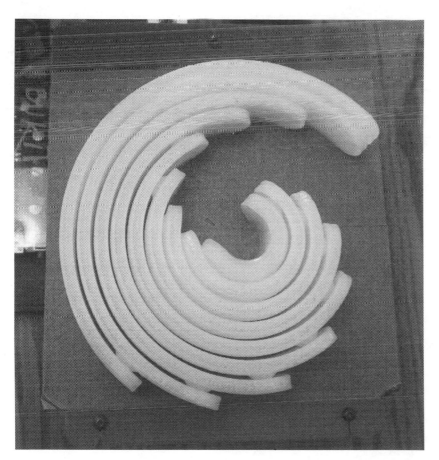

Figure 12-9. *A kinetic art piece developed by Rich as it was printed on a small printer*

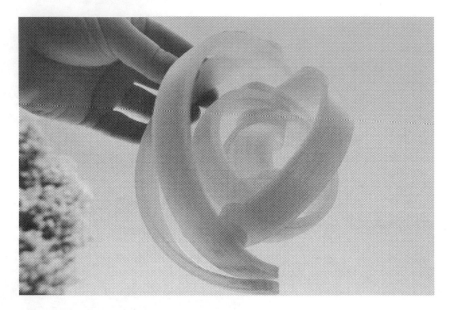

Figure 12-10. *The same piece as in Figure 12-9, but in motion. This also shows how translucent natural (undyed) PLA can be*

Educational use of 3D printing and related technologies is in its infancy. We explore these more in our book *The New Shop Class: Getting Started with 3D Printing, Arduino, and Wearable Tech* (Apress, 2015.) Being able to design a physical product is a very powerful way to enhance the teaching of subjects from theater to math.

Going Forward

We hope that you have found this book inspirational and that it has helped get you started on the road to 3D printing. Remember that in the beginning you learn more from failures than from successes, so get out there and iterate!

Summary

In this chapter you learned how to fix a few common problems and to work around some of the limitations inherent to the filament-based 3D-printing medium. We covered how to deal with prints that were too complex or physically too large, or that needed smoother surfaces than the printer alone could create. We looked at some suggestions of types of paint and glue to use, and noted some cautions about using chemical smoothing if you are new to the "shop" environment. Finally, we briefly reviewed a few topics that we did not touch on elsewhere in the book (other types of metal casting, other types of printers and applications) as a starting point for your further explorations.

APPENDIX A

∎ ∎ ∎

Supported Printer Manufacturers

The following printer manufacturers have pre-loaded settings and profiles in MatterControl as of the writing of this book. If your manufacturer is not listed here, you might check to see if they were added more recently by looking in the printer configuration menus (see Chapter 3), or see if the manufacturer says MatterControl will work with your printer.

  3D Factory

  3D Stuffmaker

  Airwolf 3D

  Blue Eagle Labs

  Deezmaker

  FlashForge (except Dreamer)

  Leapfrog

  Lulzbot

  MakerGear

  MAKEiT

  MakerBot (prior to 5th Gen)

  Me3D

  OpenBeam

  Portabee

  Printrbot

  PrintSpace

  Revolution 3D Printers

  ROBO 3D

  SeeMeCNC

  Solidoodle

  Type A Machines

  Velleman

APPENDIX B

Links

This appendix aggregates all the links in the book in one place for convenient reference. If a link appeared in more than one chapter, it is listed here under the chapter in which it appeared first.

About the Authors

Nonscriptum LLC: www.nonscriptum.com

Chapter 1: The Desktop 3D Printer

Arduino: http://arduino.cc

Indiegogo crowdfunding platform: www.indiegogo.com

Kickstarter crowdfunding platform: www.kickstarter.com

MatterHackers (creators of MatterControl): www.matterhackers.com

RepRap: for self-REPlicating RAPid prototypers: http://reprap.org

Chapter 2: What Is MatterControl?

MeshLab mesh fixing program: http://meshlab.sourceforge.net

Meshmixer app from Autodesk: www.123dapp.com/meshmixer

Chapter 3: Installing and Setting Up Matter Control

Download it: www.mattercontrol.com/#jumpMatterControlDownloads

MatterControl website: www.mattercontrol.com

MatterHackers forums: www.matterhackers.com/community/forum

MatterHackers wiki: http://wiki.mattercontrol.com

RAMBo controller driver installation instructions: www.matterhackers.com/articles/installing-rambo-driver

Chapter 4: Making a 3D Model

Autodesk 123D Catch scanning program: www.123dapp.com/catch

Autodesk: www.autodesk.com

Blender open source visual-effects development program: www.blender.org

Flat Pyramid 3D models purchase site: www.flatpyramid.com

FreeCAD CAD program: www.freecadweb.org

Instructables website: www.instructables.com

Mathematica: www.wolfram.com/mathematica/

Maya animation program: www.autodesk.com/products/maya

National Institutes of Health site for sharing methodologies and results using 3D printing: http://3dprint.nih.gov

OpenSCAD CAD program: www.openscad.org

Thingiverse printable 3D file download site: www.thingiverse.com

Tinkercad CAD program: www.tinkercad.com

TurboSquid printable 3D model purchase site: www.turbosquid.com

Yeggi, a search engine that looks at other 3D-printing model sites: www.yeggi.com

Youmagine printable 3D file download site: www.youmagine.com

Zbrush sculptural modeling program: www.zbrush.com

Chapter 5: Slicing a 3D Model – no links

Chapter 6: Controlling Your 3D Printer

Blick's art supply: www.dickblick.com

List of 3D-printer G-codes and their functions: http://reprap.org/wiki/G-code

Octoprint host program: http://octoprint.org/

Chapter 7: Material Considerations

Proto-Pasta filament manufacturer: www.proto-pasta.com

Taulman, the makers of t-glase filament: www.taulman3d.com

Chapter 8: Special Cases & Chapter 9: File and Settings Management and the Touch Table - no links

Chapter 10: Case Studies and Classroom Tips

Emmett Lalish's gear bearings: www.thingiverse.com/thing:53451

Quick-print gear bearing STL and instructions: www.youmagine.com/designs/quick-print-gear-bearing

Chapter 11: MatterControl Plugins

Plugin development instructions: http://wiki.mattercontrol.com/Developing_Plugins

Plugin repository: https://github.com/MatterHackers/MatterControlPlugins

Chapter 12: Troubleshooting and Post-Processing

XTC-3D epoxy coating: http://www.smooth-on.com/Epoxy-Coatings-XTC/c1397_1429/index.html

Index

Get the eBook for only $5!

Why limit yourself?

Now you can take the weightless companion with you wherever you go and access your content on your PC, phone, tablet, or reader.

Since you've purchased this print book, we're happy to offer you the eBook in all 3 formats for just $5.

Convenient and fully searchable, the PDF version enables you to easily find and copy code—or perform examples by quickly toggling between instructions and applications. The MOBI format is ideal for your Kindle, while the ePUB can be utilized on a variety of mobile devices.

To learn more, go to www.apress.com/companion or contact support@apress.com.